To our new friends Mavis
and Richard, enjoy Julu Phezulu.

Love from your friends
Beryl and John
x x x x x x x

Ja Boulmine 2003

Lulu Phezulu

LULU PHEZULU

Leigh Voigt's African Album

A MISCELLANY OF
PAINTINGS, CURIOSITIES,
LORE AND LEGEND
BY A BUSHVELD NATURALIST

DAVID PHILIP PUBLISHERS
1999

The author and publishers wish to acknowledge with thanks
the generous support of FIRST NATIONAL BANK
(A Division of FirstRand Bank Limited)
towards the publication of this book.

First published 1999 by David Philip Publishers (Pty) Ltd,
208 Werdmuller Centre, Newry Street, Claremont 7735,
Cape Town, South Africa

© 1999 text and illustrations Leigh Voigt

ISBN 0-86486-445-0

Design and layout by Sarah-Anne Raynham
Reproduction by Hirt and Carter, Cape Town
Printing and binding by Tien Wah, Singapore

CONTENTS

FOREWORD

'IN THE MIDST of winter I finally learned that there was in me an invincible summer': beautiful words which sum up my feelings after having read the manuscript of this highly evocative book by 'Lulu' – Leigh Voigt.

Leigh needs no introduction as her achievements as an artist and writer precede this foreword. However, if you have been fortunate enough to have had a taste of Lulu's Rex Union marmalade, then you will know something of the wisdom, knowledge and ability which await you in the pages of this wonderful book.

'Lulu' started work on the book almost twenty years ago. At the same time she was creating the illustrations for numerous other publications and was also committed to completing commissioned artworks for local and interntional collectors.

For many years I have followed and documented Leigh's accomplishments and will never cease to be delighted by her success as an artist, particularly in the international market. Her dedication and commitment are worthy of such reward and I am confident that the contents of *Lulu Phezulu* will add significantly to this achievement. While the story itself is engrossing, the subtle and highly accomplished illustrations add yet another masterly dimension.

To present Leigh is, for me, an act of pride and great pleasure. Her work as a writer and artist is of uncommon value. She has the ability to observe and scrutinise in minute detail the subject which she is documenting. This precision stems from an intense love of nature and the world at large. Many creatures defy our ability to record them accurately but Leigh has a special talent which overrides this difficulty. Her success is obvious to all who have the pleasure of its experience.

This book, like all Leigh's work, is of great importance to our heritage and knowledge, our country, its people, plants and animals. They will never be forgotten thanks to her words and illustrations.

The publishers, particularly David and Marie Philip and Russell Martin, are to be congratulated on yet another superb publication.

'Come and take choice of all my library, and so beguile thy sorrow', said Shakespeare. A sure way to 'beguile your sorrow' would be to take out and read *Lulu Phezulu*.

Steve Bales
Group Art Custodian
FNB – A division of FirstRand Bank Limited

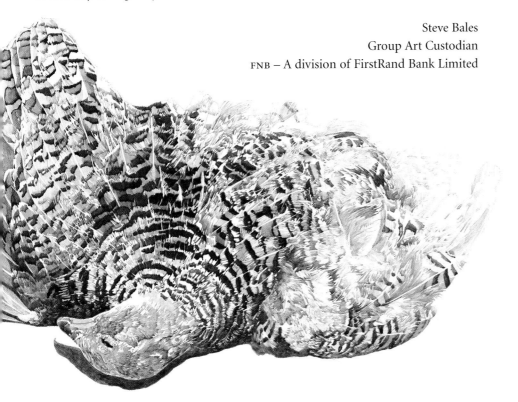

INTRODUCTION

THE HOSPITAL had tall palm trees which reached to the window of the second floor, so as I lay on the bed and waited, I watched them sway in the breeze, like spirogyra in a fish tank, except that they were on the outside and I was inside. When the pre-med pill had made me drowsy, the nurse rolled me onto a trolley and I was wheeled into a green room to await my turn on the table. The doctor's head floated into view, like an underwater monster, a grouper. He had a large black beard which was covered, as was his mass of curly black hair, with a blue shower cap to prevent dandruff from falling into my soon-to-be-opened abdomen. There were two appendicectomies and three hysterectomies scheduled for the day. I was one of the latter.

Why should it take a run-of-the-mill operation to prompt the writing of a book? Perhaps it was a symbolic milestone in a woman's life, a rite of passage, or was it because one has six weeks 'confined to bed', an immobilised body attached to a fertile imagination, sparked, no doubt, by a gram or two of pethidine? I ordered a dozen pencils, some lined writing paper and, surrounded by flowers, set to work.

The story starts where my husband, a closet architect-builder decided to build a house in the country. Our children were still small, so it was with mixed feelings of excitement and trepidation that we bought a piece of wild Africa and left the city. I chose to write about things

The home we built is on top of a mountain and we named it 'Lulu phezulu'. My nickname is Lulu and phezulu *is Zulu for 'on top'.*

in nature that are personal to me, and as a result this book is by no means comprehensive. I take a look, with an artist's playful eye, at birth and death, sex and violence, unusual behaviour, adaptations, symbiotic relationships and that indefinable spiritual connection between Man and Beast. Many superstitions and customs adhere to us, but their origins are all rooted in scientific reasoning. Without these taboos or beliefs we would catch diseases, be struck by lightning, be bitten by snakes, remain unmarried, lose our loved ones or our way.

I make no excuse for using photographs as reference for some of my paintings – most wildlife artists do, even if they say they don't. The difference lies in what to select from that photograph, what to put in, what to leave out. To copy a photograph slavishly is as boring to the artist as to the viewer. But if what attracts the artist's attention is a certain something special, then the duty of the artist is to recognise it, capture it on paper and present it.

Reviews of specialist natural history books written by ologists of all the sciences evoke the most meticulous of critics' scrutiny, and my stomach sinks with the thinking of it. This book is just something I needed to do.

The path is beset with danger and delight. I hope you will be absorbed, amused and occasionally astonished.

Amavuhlandlela! *

* Swazi greeting which means 'Go well, travel with pleasurable dalliance'.

DEDICATED TO MY PARENTS
BARBARA JEPPE AND DR CARL JEPPE

chapter one

In the **Beginning**

Bird's nest on lace cloth

W E MADE OUR WAY up the old wagon trail which once was the main road from Lydenburg to the coast. Near the top of the hill the track took a sharp turn to the left where the clearing was covered with tall yellow grass. John stopped the bakkie and we climbed out. Through the gnarled branches of the kiaat trees, the Crocodile River could be seen, reflecting the blue of the sky. Harry walked silently to the edge of the cliff. John followed him and pointed out the small railway station, the distant radio receiving tower and the neighbours' boundaries.

It was to the distant blue mountains that my gaze turned, a view of the African bush, which was as it was, before Man trod heavily upon the Earth.

It was August and the bush was dry. Some aloes were in flower, their orange inflorescences dotting the hillsides. The delicate tracery of winter thornveld is one of the quintessential images that those born of Africa carry with them for the whole of their lives.

I bent and fingered the earth. It was hard yellow *ouklip* with hardly any topsoil and the heel of my shoe barely made an impression. A horsefly buzzed near my ear. I walked to the edge where the men stood. Harry still had not said a word. He had an expression on his face and a set to his jaw that was unfamiliar to me. In that moment I realised to my horror that this was where he had decided to build our house. Here. On the top of this *vaal*-coloured mountain, no electricity, no schools, no shops, hundreds of kilometres from our friends and family.

The fundamental requirement was, of course, water. The source of the stream was a natural spring high up in the kloof and seemed strong enough to provide enough crystal-clear water for general household use, but required a bit of creative engineering to get it to the proposed site.

A reliable engine and pump were installed amidst the delicate maidenhair ferns on the loamy banks. When the engine thudded into noisy activity for the first time I was horrified by the rainbow oil slick in the reservoir and the diesel fumes.

We will never forget the day that water gushed from the roughly constructed outlet. Harry, whose emotions rarely exceeded a blink or a sigh, removed his shirt and hopped up and down and raised his hands as if in praise of a miracle. A pioneering spirit danced enthusiastically in the air.

The presence of a buffelsdoring (Ziziphus mucronata) in the area indicated subterranean water but the depth of rock precluded any borehole drilling.

The love of dirt is amongst the earliest of passions, as it is the latest. Mud pies gratify one of our first and best instincts. So long as we are dirty we are pure. Fondness for the ground comes back to a man after he has run the round of pleasure and business, eaten dirt, and sown wild oats, drifted about the world and taken the wind of all its moods. The love of digging in the ground (or of looking on while he pays another to dig) is as sure to come back to him as he is sure, at last, to go under the ground and stay there. To own a bit of ground, to scratch it with a hoe, to plant seeds, and watch their renewal of life – this is the commonest delight of the race, the most satisfying thing a man can do.
— CHARLES DUDLEY WARNER

And on the second day we laboured, and the third, and all the days thereafter.

Our first breakfast was cooked on a small gas stove under the flap of a two-man pup tent. We produced a lavish spread of freshly squeezed orange juice, fried eggs and bacon, herbed tomatoes, toast and jam. The sun had been up for only a few hours and already the sweat poured off our faces and our shirts clung to our bodies. The foundations were only a few inches deep. I jumped aside when a spider the size of my hand scuttled into the shade of my skirt. The flies buzzed and ants were attracted to scraps on the plates. The white tablecloth I had laid out on the bare ground with ceremonial panache was now full of stickiness and sand.

Within a few weeks we had progressed from a pup tent to a relatively comfortable wooden pondokkie which Harry had knocked up out of some split poles. It had a corrugated-iron roof and was to be our home until the main house was completed. I regarded it with immense pride. It consisted of a living room, that is, a kitchen/dining/sitting/work room, about the size of an average bathroom, and a closed-off section with two raised bunk-beds and hooks on the walls to hang things on.

We had very little storage space, so we bought supplies carefully and nothing was ever wasted. But we encountered another problem. We could not keep anything cold. Harry is partial to a cold beer in the evening. He devised a canvas cooler, which, when filled with water and hung in the breeze in the shade of a fig tree, kept the butter from melting and the meat from rotting.

The children learnt to be unafraid of the dark, the spiders and even the snakes. In fact children are naturals when it comes to nature. They played in the mud, they laid out cities in the sand, they tended beetles and went off with their spade and paper roll to poo in the dark.

We had satisfied ourselves that schooling was not a problem. There was a junior boarding school an hour's drive away, which, with special permission, meant three nights at home and four at school. We liked the family atmosphere at the small school and were content in the knowledge that the children were always happy there. The school principal was a rather special person who, when I asked if we could take the children out of school for ten days to go on a trip overseas, replied: 'Of course, my dear, you must not let school interfere with their education.'

But, as all children do, especially boys, they complained about the food. I nearly

believed them, when, one Monday morning on the way to school, we drove behind a tractor towing a trailer piled high with half-loaves of stale bread. Our jokes about 'there goes breakfast!' were all but confirmed when the tractor turned off into the school road just ahead of us. With relief we discovered that there was a pig farm adjacent to the school grounds.

To teach the children not to tell fibs and at the same time inform them about the phases of the moon, they were told the story of the hare. It's an old Khoikhoi legend and goes as follows:

The moon sent a louse to tell the people not to worry if they saw it slowly disappear, for it will surely return in a cycle, and in the same way, so will people die and live again. But the lazy louse lingered and on his way told the story to a quick brown hare, who said

At that stage, the only thing I knew about rabbits was that their skulls made the best glue.

he would carry the message to the people. *When he got to earth he told them that when they died, that would be the end of them. When the moon heard about this gross inaccuracy he was very angry and seized a piece of wood and hit the hare on the lip. Ever since then the hare has a cleft lip.*

My children listened intently but wanted to know where the moon suddenly got a piece of wood from. I'm sure the point of the story was lost on them.

Dragonflies are said to have been sent by Satan to cause mischief in the world, often being called Devil's darning needles – in Afrikaans, *naaldekoker*. Children are told that if they tell lies the devil's darning needle will sew up their mouths, even likely to sew up noses and ears and go right on through the head. It will also sew up the mouths of scolding women and cursing men and has the whimsical habit of sewing together the toes of anyone it finds sleeping uncovered.

Every morning we woke before sunrise. The valley was peaceful and soft, gently tinged with pink and orange, the mist still clinging to the foothills of the distant

Every morning I raked the sand floor.

The split pole walls let in shafts of light, lizards and draft.

Steps to the lavatory, called the Lava Tree.

I regarded our little pondokkie with immense pride.

mountains. When the sun rose, sharp shafts of light created deeper shadows, the breeze came up and the temperature curiously dropped.

The typically African smell of early morning wood-fires signalled the rising of the labourers. We had to employ two or three people to help dig the foundations, mix the cement and lay the heavy concrete blocks. Once coffee had been brewed, the working day began.

Things did not always go smoothly. Our first storm was such an event.

The Payne's Grey clouds hung like dense dark grapes. The air was ominously still and warm. Not a leaf fluttered. My young son, Walter, gently slipped his hand into mine. Then an impatient wind tugged at my skirt and drops of rain began to spot the dry ochre earth. The trees bent, the monkeys screamed. Thunder and lightning crashed around us. Everyone rushed to tie things down, to cover, collect, to prepare for the storm. The air grew suddenly cooler and filled with the smell of moist earth. We sought shelter in our flimsy dwelling as the wind rattled the corrugated-iron roof. A shelf of medicines crashed to the ground and a pile of books had to be covered with a sheet of plastic when the hook fastener of the door snapped and rain came in at right angles. The noise on the roof was deafening as the wind competed with hail to create missiles of metal and ice. Harry ordered the children to get under the bunks. Water sprayed through the slatted wooden walls and we were drenched. A huge volume of liquid yellow soil came gushing down the slope, oozed through the gaps and swirled round our ankles. Walter showed the whites of his eyes under the bed.

Walter, let me remind you, is our son, not the dog.

In our thirsty land where water is vital, it is not surprising that mystique surrounds thunder. In the rural areas of KwaZulu-Natal it is believed that there are two types of thunder. The male thunder is long, deep, drawn-out rumbling, without lightning or hail. It is generally heard at some distance, as a murmuring sound, becoming increasingly loud as it approaches. This kind of thunder is not feared, although it is looked upon with much awe and respect. The female thunder is sudden and cracking thunder, accompanied by forked lightning and very heavy rainfall, often with hail.

Some Zulus describe the sky as having a dark dome with perpetual light beyond, and the stars as small holes through which the light glimmers at night. Nkosi is the

Winter grasses

The blue-bird carries the sky on his back.
— HENRY DAVID THOREAU

Great Creator and when his cattle are driven to the grazing ground in the sky after rain, they tramp through the mud putting their hooves through the floor of the sky, letting the light shine through. The Milky Way is the main entrance to the cattle enclosure. Falling stars are caused when cattle are clumsy and drag a foot, so that the light is seen before the mud fills in again.

When asked about earthquakes, some Zulus explain that the sky is a huge rock, blue in colour, which stretches from one end of the flat surface of the earth to the other. The great vault of rock rests on the edges of the earth, while the earth itself, being flat, is held up by four bulls, 'carrying the earth on their horns. When one of them shakes its head, then the earth also shakes.'

Our technology is not yet able to detect precisely when an earthquake will occur but in 1969 all the animals in the zoo in Tientsin in China became agitated simultaneously two hours before a huge earthquake struck. A warning was issued based on their behaviour.

In Tashkent, in the former Soviet Republic of Uzbekistan, in 1966, an hour before an earthquake, the residents watched a mass migration of ants carrying their eggs.

In February 1975, two whole days before a great earthquake struck Haicheng, China, pigs fought each other frantically in their pens, some biting off other pigs' tails.

As any golfer will tell you, to shelter under trees when lightning threatens is foolish to say the least, but certain trees are reputed to be efficacious in warding off lightning. A twig from the Natal or Safsaf Willow, *Salix mucronata* var. *woodii*, coated with the fat of a black goat and thrust into the thatch of a hut whilst another twig is pointed towards the threatening thunderclouds, is sure to redirect the storm. But if crocodile fat is at hand and lightning threatens, seek out a *Celtis africana* (White Stinkwood) and use as above. The smelly Stink Shepherd's tree (*Boscia foetida*) will also do the trick but it is hard on the nose. The rare *Umtiza listerana* grows in the Transkei and is

now a protected species; however, pieces of bark are still hung in huts as protection against lightning.

If all these measures fail, there is a strict code of conduct regarding the burial of someone struck by lightning. The corpse has to be buried in the same clothes he or she was wearing when struck, without a coffin or other wrapping. Burial in red soil must be avoided at all costs. 'Red earth is hot, it makes the man even hotter. Then he will simply burn and there will be no rainfall.' The body should not be buried deep, so that the right arm of the corpse can be raised and kept in position with earth, the forefinger allowed to stick out of the earth, so that the people may see where he has gone.

Like thunder, rain too has gender. Soft gentle rain is referred to as female rain whilst hard pelting rain is male.

Although a wondrous sight after a storm, to some of the people of Africa the rainbow is malignant and dangerous. Coming so soon after rain, it is believed to have caused the stopping of the rain. It is also believed that to point at the rainbow will result in the finger becoming stiff. Strangely enough, in England, to point at a rainbow is also regarded as dreadfully unlucky.

But back home the storm had set us back a few days. There was no structural damage to the main house, though some of our cement had got wet, the road was washed away, and all our belongings were soggy. The paintings I had just finished and pinned to the wall had been torn, soaked and badly damaged.

Next morning, to recover my sense of humour, I walked along the little path kicking a stone here, absently breaking a twig there. The sun warmed my back and a cow bellowed in the distance. Soon milk cans would start clanking and my private reverie would become a reality of hot porridge, bacon and eggs. I faced the fullness of the sun and, closing my eyes, stood still for a moment and drew in a deep breath of sweet damp air. The earth was soft and dark underfoot and dewdrops sparkled in the sunlight. Even the birds didn't know I was there, or didn't mind. A little quick brown one landed on a branch just above my head. For that brief second we were equals. The little brown bird and I. We had survived the storm.

When the walls of the house were shoulder-height I began to feel that this move was not such a bad idea after all. As winter approached the weather cooled but the veg-

etation was still green and lush. The perilous road had become well hardened by constant use. We had thought we could move in before the cold weather set in, but with constant setbacks it was not to be so. Our wooden pondokkie would have to suffice. We nailed bits of carpeting and layers of newspaper to the walls to seal the spaces between the split poles and put grass matting on the bare earth floor.

As the food of the veld became less for all nature's little creatures, nature's little creatures discovered us. The rats and mice launched a total onslaught into our provisions. They plundered the soap, the rubber gloves, the gramophone records. They became very bold. I lay on my bunk at night and watched them stand on their hind legs and peer into boxes. I had a horror of them scurrying up my nightie and nibbling on my tender parts, so I determined to get rid of them. That wasn't so easy. Not for a confirmed conservationist. Poison was out. Pellet guns are unwieldy in bed and useless in the dark. Eventually we adopted the simple but tedious habit of not leaving a scrap of food around and we packed all our things into tin trunks. Later, when the house was finished, we got a cat.

The first time we encountered a snake in the house the children were sent to a place of safety, that is, on the roof. Harry and I donned crash helmets, lowered the visors and, armed with brooms, advanced. After two hours we were exhausted, but the snake was vanquished, that is to say, gently squashed against the wall. Not wanting to kill him or even hurt him we had used the soft end of the broom. We put him into a box and exported him to Lydenburg. Then we sat down to wait for his mate.

There is a superstition that if you kill a snake, its mate will seek you out and kill you. In the years that followed, his mate came, his friends came, his friends' mates came. They never harmed us and we never harmed them. The belief stems, I suppose, from the fact that snakes are often found in pairs, particularly during the mating season. If one is killed, chances are its mate will be in the same area. Anything that instils fear in man is usually shrouded in superstition.

'It may seem simple or obvious that if you want to pop a snake into a bag, the best way of doing it is to put your hand in the bag first, grab the snake, then turn the bag inside out quickly, so that now your hand's on the outside and the snake's on the inside.'

— IONIDES

Along the east coast of Mozambique and Maputaland, the Tsonga carry the powdered ashes of a snake in a little bag around their necks to guard against being bitten by a snake.

The cure in Greece is a 'snake-stone', ground to a powder and sprinkled on the site of a bite. The Zulus, in common with Swedes, believe that snakes are household gods. For Zulus it is *idlozi*, which lives in the fences around their kraals. It is considered harmless and no one is allowed to injure it. If it is killed or injured, terrible things are sure to happen to the inhabitants and their relatives.

The Vine or Twig Snake is poisonous, reportedly able to launch an attack from a branch, its spear-shaped head completely penetrating its victim. There is, fortunately, a cure, consisting of the application of a drop of blood from someone who, legend insists, must be one of twins.

Democritus, the ancient Greek philosopher, stated that snakes were generated from the mixed blood of certain birds and that whoever ate a snake would understand the language of birds.

Misconceptions abound regarding the burning of a dead python. In South Africa heavy rains will result, whereas in Zimbabwe the country will suffer the consequences of a long drought. Another misconception is that they hypnotise their prey before striking. It is simply that snakes have no eyelids, which accounts for their unblinking gaze.

The Mozambique Spitting Cobra, known locally as *imfezi*, has an awesome reputation. 'It travels only at night, so the story goes, and then only along the tops of trees. So swiftly does it move that if there are no more trees nearby, its lair is instantly recognisable by the sight of dead animals at the base of its tree. These and other victims are supposedly killed instantly by the snake's poisonous breath, the victim turning black after death.' This belief stems from the fact that the *imfezi* is a very dangerous snake, 'spitting' its venom accurately into the eyes of its victim three or four metres away. It is exceedingly quick, lunging forward, exhaling sharply with a loud hiss.

At our home, Lulu Phezulu, we have in summer many red toads, *Schismaderma carens*. They live behind bookcases, in drawers and under cupboards. One day the smell of something dead came from the chest of drawers in which I keep my clothes.

Imfezi, *Mozambique Spitting Cobra.*

I opened the bottom drawer and pulled out a fringed scarf to which was attached a dead and mangled red toad. Its body, with its claws still clinging to the fringe, was covered, along with 30 cm of scarf, with drying snake spit. In disgust I pulled out the whole drawer, got down on my hands and knees, and peered into the cavity, right into the unblinking gaze of a Mozambique Spitting Cobra.

When I had recovered my composure and washed off my spectacles we caught the snake, put him in a box and took him by car to a suitable place at least ten kilometres away, wondering just how long he had been living a life of luxury, surrounded by cashmere and silk.

The supposed healing properties of snakes are as diverse as they are unproven.

In ancient England a woman in labour used to be girded with the sloughed skin of a snake in order to be quickly delivered of her child. Some people believed that putting snake skins in their hats cured headaches; others applied adder skins to embedded thorns, believing this would draw them out.

To my mind the snake, twined around rods, symbolising the medical profession, is hardly reassuring.

Some nights were so misty and damp that sleeping in the car with the children was preferable to my pondok bunk bed. But when sleep just wouldn't come, the dark hours found me huddled over a spluttering gas lamp with a hot-water bottle on my lap and an eiderdown round my shoulders. Trying to complete some paintings I was bedevilled by the moths attracted to the light. As a great furry moth blundered into my smoothly applied watercolour wash, leaving a trail of fluffy scales and bits of legs and things, it would have to be clamped under an upturned glass or cup or mug. I was in no mood to be impressed by its beauty. The physical exertion of the day's building operations ensured Harry a well-deserved and good night's sleep. For my part, I felt utterly abandoned when he fell asleep. But out of those lonely pre-dawn mist-shrouded nights, when the eerie hoot of an owl or the hysterical screech of a bushbaby was my only companion, there came an awareness of the senses which gave me a feeling of exquisite peace and solitude.

As the days grew longer and the nights warmer and the house nearer the habitable stage, my excitement increased. The dried grass in the yoghurt jar was replaced by spring flowers. The floor was diligently raked every morning and the grocery cupboard turned out and re-stocked. The hillside, instead of appearing tangled and hostile, softened. Spring had sprung.

I became aware of persistent bird calls. A mournful wailing whistle, which went on all through the night and well into the misty morning, puzzled us for many weeks. We asked questions and got answers such as: it's a chameleon, a monitor lizard, a puff adder. It was, in fact,

a Buff-spotted Flufftail. A flufftail, being a member of the crake family, spends most of its time in the dense vegetation down by the river. If disturbed, it will quickly scuttle away rather than fly. At sunset it may climb into a bush, not more than two metres off the ground, and call. The call is ventriloquial, so it is usually difficult to locate its source and, of course, even more difficult in the dark. They are small decorative birds with buff-coloured heads and spotty fluffy tails. The females are spotty all over. They lay their eggs in nests with little lids carefully concealed amongst the tangled vegetation of the forest floor. The parents can be extraordinarily bold in the defence of their nest, even attacking one's legs, assuming one has got one's legs through the dense impenetrable undergrowth in the dark.

I think, and therefore I am, responsible for the extinction of the last Buff-spotted Flufftail in our valley. Early one morning I was driving at quite a speed alongside the river on the main tar road, when a bird flew up out of the grass. Cursing, I looked in my rearview mirror but seeing no flurry of feathers I assumed it had flown away. A few days later I was washing the car and found the shrivelled carcass of a female Buff-spotted Flufftail, in perfect condition, stuck to the radiator, and I present her to you here. R.I.P.

Understanding the 'language' of the land is essential if your sheep are to flourish. Archie, a farmer friend in the Karoo, listens to his lucerne. He holds a few leaves between his thumb and forefinger and, raising his hand to his ear, he gently rubs the leaves together and, closing his eyes, he listens intently. It is at a certain hour of a certain day when the sap has risen to a point that harvesting is critical.

Earlier, I was talking about people scrambling about in the dark, to ferret out birds. Well, the Black Cuckoo needs no seeking out. Come spring, it can drive sleepless farmers to distraction causing them, as Ken Newman says, to 'chase about in their pyjamas armed with a shotgun'. The mournful 'I feel s-i-i-i-i-ck' carries monotonously on throughout the days and into the nights. The fact is that the same farmer was, a few short weeks before, overjoyed to hear the distinctive call of the harbinger of the first spring rains. The Piet-my-vrou also announces the coming of the rains. His three-note call rings out his message and once words have been put to his simple melody you cannot get them out of your head. 'Piet-my-vrou, Piet-my-vrou, Piet-my-vrou.' If I could only persuade my seasonal residents, the Piet-my-vrou (Red-chested Cuckoo) and the Black Cuckoo, that their presence has been noted and that their territories will be respected and that they need no longer assail my ears and fray my nerves with their repetitive calls.

When the call of the European Cuckoo is heard by peasants in Germany, those who have money in their pockets turn it over to ensure plenty more in the future and general good luck. In fact the call of the cuckoo has more oracular powers than any other. It prophesies the hour of the day, the numbers of years of life and how long a maiden will remain unmarried.

To interpret these signs is impossible. To tell which time span relates to which question and to which number of calls per hour is only for those who understand Cuckoospeak. However, its message is clear to the adulterer, for the cuckoo has a habit of laying its eggs in other birds' nests. The word 'cuckold' is thus derived.

If the Rufous-naped Lark, which is purported to be the best singer, is sitting in a tree and calling, it is a sign of rain, but if the bird rises into the air, calling and singing, imitating all kinds of birds, then a hailstorm can be expected.

In Great Britain, rural people generally recommend drinking three larks' eggs to acquire a sweet singing voice. Perhaps that's why the term *rooinek* (derogatory for 'English-man') used to be connected to the Rufous-naped Lark.

During one of my walks in the forest I looked up; a flash of scarlet and green caught my eye. In the dappled canopy, the jewel of the forest went about catching insects with agile twists and turns in mid-flight. For this glorious bird, timid and elusive, the romantic Frenchman François le Vaillant recalled his Khoikhoi paramour and named it the Narina Trogon. The word Nerine is derived

Narina Trogon

> To a person uninstructed in natural history, his country or seaside stroll is a walk through a gallery filled with wonderful works of art, nine-tenths of which have their faces turned towards the wall.
>
> — T.H. HUXLEY

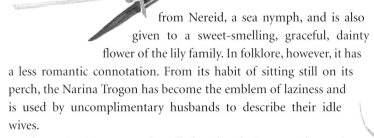

Fiscal Shrike

When you see a group of White Helmetshrikes, you will soon see someone you haven't seen for a long time. It is regarded by the hunters of Zimbabwe as a bird of good omen.

from Nereid, a sea nymph, and is also given to a sweet-smelling, graceful, dainty flower of the lily family. In folklore, however, it has a less romantic connotation. From its habit of sitting still on its perch, the Narina Trogon has become the emblem of laziness and is used by uncomplimentary husbands to describe their idle wives.

The Narina Trogon can be called up by playing recordings of its call. Highly territorial during breeding season, it will investigate any intruder. A number of people call it up by cupping their hands together and blowing seven soft hoots. A spishing sound, made by clasping one's hands over one's mouth to make a small sound chamber, pressing one's tongue against the teeth and hissing in short sharp bursts, also brings this curious bird closer, or any curious bird for that matter.

Spishing is supposed to imitate the distress call of the Fiscal Shrike, although why that should elicit any sympathy I fail to understand. After all, the Fiscal Shrike is a sadistic little fellow, hanging his corpses on meat hooks. It's also a pugnacious bird (alias Jackie Hanger, Butcher Bird), on record as having killed a Common Egg-eater Snake 53 cm long and weighing 33 grams.

The Bokmakierie, *Telephorus zeylonus*, which is also a shrike, has, in common with most other shrikes, the telephonic call with its mate. Its place in folklore is twofold. Where the bird habitually calls is considered a good place for a cattle kraal, and when a bird does call it indicates that the cattle will increase. It is also considered a rain bird, in that, in times of drought, if one is killed and put in water, rain will fall.

One of nature's more successful creations, the owl, has undeservedly attracted a bad press and a rotten reputation. For something whose night vision is two or three times greater than ours, who can hear a mouse in a distant donga, and whose silent wing beats caress the night air to take its prey by surprise, does not deserve the notorious label of Evil Omen. Granted, to be looked at by an owl is a withering experience.

Its piercing stare, devoid of warmth and humour, is challenging, accusing. When satisfied that the object of his attention is worthless, his lids lower and his gaze withdraws with weary contempt. The hoot of an owl sends a chill down the straightest of spines. In East Africa the hooting of an owl in the night is particularly disastrous for a baby. If the child grows up with an illness or defect, the Swahili people say *ameliliwa*, 'the child has been hooted over'. If an owl hoots as it flies over a hut or, worse still, settles on the roof, it is regarded as a messenger of death. If a person imitates the cry of an owl all his blankets will be burned, suggesting, euphemistically, that death and disaster are all around.

If a bird flies into the house, it is a forerunner of important news. Some say it is a sign of death, especially if it cannot get out again; and if it is a white bird it is a sure sign of death. If a woodpecker taps on the house, it brings bad news, often news of a death in the family. In the United States, hearing an owl hooting signifies bad luck.

Peacock feathers are very unlucky; they prevent girls from marrying and babies from being born.

It is also a general belief throughout the United States that it is bad to have designs of bird decorations on wedding presents, for the happiness of the newly weds will all the sooner take wing, whereas in China a pair of geese are often given as a wedding present because geese are said to be faithful to one another.

It is bad luck to kill a stork. In Morocco, if a stork builds on the roof, the house will become empty, but in Germany and Austria it is a good sign. In Germany it is said that a stork flying over the house presages a birth. The belief was that storks picked up infants from marshes, ponds, wells, springs and lakes, where the souls of unborn children dwell. It is also said that if storks leave their nests and build others hurriedly in trees, it is a sign of war; they have also been known to leave a whole area

Bokmakierie

Emerald-spotted Dove

before pestilence struck, and if they leave their nests forever, great calamity is foreseen.

The beautiful but insecure Tambourine Dove, or *isibhelu*, says, 'Wherever I lay my eggs I get robbed of them, wherever I lay my eggs I get robbed of them, until I feel my heart drop, drop, drop, drop … ' This makes no sense whatsoever considering that the frail platform of twiglets that hardly passes for a nest is very difficult to find.

Another bird which presents with paranoid tendencies, always nervous and edgy, is the Emerald-spotted Dove, which has a similar-sounding call though a different interpretation has been placed upon it. 'My mother is dead! My father is dead! All my relations are dead! Oh! Oh! Oh! Oh! Oh! … '

Each time I hear it, it seems to me to be saying, 'Rule, Britannia, Britannia rules the waves, poo! poo! poo! poo! poo! … '

The White-throated Robin makes the first call in the morning, his joyful tumble of notes urging you to get up; he is the local gossip, the morning 'newsman' announcing all that happened during the night. Then at the end of the long day, the robin is the last to turn in, dutifully reporting on all that happened during the day.

The onomatopoeic call of the hadeda, *inkankane*, is one of the most evocative sounds of the early morning and late afternoon. Though, beware, for to imitate its call will surely cause you to break out in boils on your seat. And when many hadedas are continually flying above they are telling of a rich harvest.

As I write, a lovesick Purple-crested Lourie hurls himself at his reflection in my studio window, and the mess around the side mirror of my Kombi tells me that a Chin-spot Batis has been duelling his rival.

The Quail Finch (*Ortygospiza atricollis*) is a small ground-loving bird and quite difficult to see, sitting still as you pass, and only if you are about to step on it will it fly away. Its Zulu name is *unkonklwe*, recalling the sound it makes as it rises. Because of its reluctance to fly it is considered a lazy bird. But it is a devoted parent, both the male and the female taking turns to incubate the eggs, and sometimes you may see

White-throated Robin

The Purple-crested
Lourie, igwalagwala *(the sound echoes
its call)*, is a shy forest-dwelling bird, which,
when it makes a particular cry, foretells the death
of a buck by the hunter, though the animal will escape if
the bird remains silent. It has brilliant red wing feathers
worn as head ornaments only by noblemen and kings, which is
ironic because igwala *actually means coward.*

them sitting together, side by side. If it is startled while sitting on eggs it will fly away reluctantly, but silently; that's when one knows to search for the nest nearby. If it is not breeding, however, it will vocalise immediately and loudly ... uNkonklwe! ... uNkonklwe!

The fragile domed nest is made of grass, by the male, on the ground, between two tufts of grass, always with a yard or patch of bare ground at the entrance. This clearing is known as the bird's playground or dance-floor. Its purpose could be to have a clear view of the area to spot approaching predators; or for courtship displays by the male; or as a 'landing strip' for birds coming to the nest.

Stories abound in the Transkei of the female Quail Finch dribbling an egg from the nest and lying down on her back in her yard, tossing the egg into the air with her feet, then skilfully catching it again. I personally have never observed this fanciful behaviour but am prepared to enjoy the image. After the eggs hatch, it is said that she puts the chicks on the playground and plays with them. In fact, the chicks leave the nest reluctantly and seldom venture far from home.

Like us.

In English lore a white feather is a sign of cowardice in wartime, but a single tail feather of the majestic Blue Crane, bird emblem of South Africa, is worn as a sign of the highest office by the proud monarch of the Zulu nation, King Goodwill Zwelithini.

Quail Finch

chapter two

In
the
Past

THE HOUSE was taking shape magnificently, so when not needed 'on site' or to provide meals I took walks in the hills or down to the stream. A whole new world opened up to me. I went on journeys of discovery, into a new world, a metre at a time.

My first love affair was with a lizard. He had never seen a human before and therefore did not know to be frightened of me. I was sitting very still on a flat rock when he saw me. He turned his head this way and that, his little heart beating visibly in his midriff. He had a big grin on his face and seemed eager to make friends. I sat even stiller. He became more curious. He walked along my foot, stopped when he got to my knee, looked at me again, smiled, turned and went on his way.

I ventured into the hills as often as possible, collecting specimens to draw.

On one occasion, there had been a recent veld fire and all the stones were exposed. I had thought that our hills, with a stream running through them, would have been a good valley for Stone Age Man to have chosen to make his home. The rock was mainly dolomite and shale, not normally used by Stone Age Man for making his weapons. But on this particular day, O Glorious Day, with black tufts of burnt grass crunching deliciously beneath my feet, I found the one and only artefact I have ever found on our own land. It was a perfect handaxe. I cradled it in the palm of my hand. It was made from a very different type of rock from that of the area and therefore I concluded that it was probably carried by a lone ranger 40 000 years ago and discarded, for reasons we shall never know, on the very hillside on which I chose to collect pink fire lilies for my yoghurt jar. I imagined this pre-supermarket man, naked, shoulders stooped, feet calloused, arms scarred and scratched, nimbly making his way between the rocks, his beady little eyes darting this way and that, searching, alert.

There are caves in the distant mountains, large sheltering rock overhangs, sparkling waterfalls, alongside grassy plains which, thousands of years ago, teemed with game. A family group, the nuclear family of yesteryear (the only difference being that grandpa was probably eaten before his 30th birthday), existed in blissful surroundings, notwithstanding the leopards and mosquitoes.

How does one tell the difference between an artefact, that is, a stone tool purposefully made by man, and an eolith or ventrifact, which is a natural broken-off flake

If, on your travels, you see a pile of stones, obviously intentionally heaped, the stones at all levels being well coloured with lichens, suggesting that they have been there for a great length of time, do not pass it by without adding a stone of your own. It is a cairn, known as isivivane in Zulu and means 'travel well', a monument to the ancestors. Make a silent request and implore, 'Generations of the past, watch over us!'

THE GRINDING STONE

Daily grain is ground
On a granite grinding stone
STONE GROUND GRAIN
(The fashion in smart shops)
But from the ground
Where grain is grown
It never stops
It never stops.
Again and again,
around and around,
It never stops.
Grow your grain
Store your grain
Grind your grain,
Makes an agonising sound,
An agonising sound.
Groan, grain,
Ground grain,
Grain grown
Groan grind
Groan grain
Groan again.

LEIGH VOIGT

caused by heat or rock falls? The type of rock used by Stone Age Man or Bushman was usually dense, homogeneous and flint-like. Striking one rock with another produced a flaking-off of a piece, always generally consistent with the next flake, only different perhaps in size, depending on the angle or the strength of the blow. The fractured face of the flake is easily recognisable. The struck platform is usually at 120° to the now exposed face. At the point of impact the surface is swollen into what is called a bulb of percussion, sometimes showing small stress striations or vertical fissures, and almost without exception displaying a bulbar scar, a flat oval depression, as if a little chip has fallen off.

If the maker was happy with the result of his first blow he would continue to refine the tool by making secondary workings along its sides, chipping off more little flakes to produce a good cutting edge. The side of the handaxe invariably has an elongated S shape.

Holding a near perfect handaxe or arrowhead in my hand, I can't help feeling that hundreds of thousands of years ago, man must have derived aesthetic and proud pleasure from having created something better than the next man.

Which reminds me, the house was getting on beautifully.

The grinding stone, upon which the daily grain was ground, and around which the women gathered, was the focal point of the kraal and therefore a symbol of family unity. If the kraal had to be abandoned, the grinding stone was always left behind; it was bad luck to transport it to a new place. The new residents would take over the stone as if it were their own.

Of all the myths, legends or beliefs, none is more fundamental to our existence than that of our origin as a human race. Setting aside the scientific evidence we can indulge in fanciful metaphorical and spiritual sources for our creation. The Bible tells of Adam and Eve, but the Baronga, a branch of the Tsonga, believe that 'one man and one woman suddenly came out from a reed, which exploded and there they were!'

A reed-bed is *umhlanga* in Zulu, but I can hardly reconcile today's seaside holiday resort of Umhlanga Rocks on the north coast of Natal with the Cradle of Mankind.

I have an infallible remedy for melancholia. I listen to either Handel's 'Largo' or Ravel's Boléro and realise that both composers must, at some time, have been more depressed than me. The thought always cheers me up. I also take walks.

On one such walk I came upon a depression of a different kind, a spoor I had not seen before. Most of our books were still in storage and I could not look it up, so I satisfied my curiosity by tracking the creature myself. The tracks were in the soft earth at the side of the road and every now and again they disappeared into the grass, only to reappear twenty metres or so further on. It was neither a buck spoor nor a cat track, so had me really puzzled. When the tracks veered off along a distinct game trail I followed them. Darwin once said that Africa has more dangerous beasts than any other continent. I was sure half of them lived at the other end of my pathway. In many places I had to crawl on all fours, taking comfort therein, that the beast must be smaller than me. It may be smaller but there may be many! The trail was obviously well used, the grass was flattened and the pathway clearly defined. I found a wealth of clues as to what uses the path; a sloughed snake skin, crab shells with legs missing, rocks that had been recently turned over, a tuft of fur caught on a thorn, a pile of droppings like a string of black beads, an owl pellet and a cat scat and, at last, a porcupine quill.

It was the beginning of my second love affair, this time with a most unusual fellow.

Porcupines are nocturnal, shy and smelly; and dangerous when cornered. I did find one eventually, or rather the dogs did; they cornered one in its lair and there was a lot of barking and rattling of quills.

The Porcupine is a vegetarian, yet gnaws on bones as a source of calcium and phosphates. In a lair in the Kalahari Gemsbok Park were found Gemsbok horns, bones, tortoise shells, pieces of wood, iron bars, rusty cans and enamel mugs. One would think that the reason for the Porcupine's strong smell is its contact with rotten bones but in fact it's due to a far more unsavoury habit. During courtship the male Porcupine creates an odour bond with his mate by approaching her on his hind legs and spraying her with urine. Mounting occurs daily throughout the year and constant physical contact between males and females is required to maintain regular ovarian activity.

~

The illegal trade in rhino horn and elephant ivory pales into insignificance when one compares the prices of those items with the products of the Porcupine. The dried carcass of a Porcupine is worth several hundred American dollars, and the gallstones

Hedgehog

half a million dollars a kilo. But please don't go out and decimate the Porcupine population. You would have to kill a huge number of Porcupines to find out if they even had any gallstones.

In tribal areas Porcupines were once highly regarded as royal game and any slaughtered animal had to be taken whole to the chief, where the quills were removed and the carcass gutted. In return, the chief would reward the presenter with a chicken.

I am told that to catch a Porcupine bare-handed is not impossible. There is a region of long hairs extending well beyond the quills, at the end of the tail. If, when the tail is motionless, you seize these hairs suddenly in one hand and pull firmly, the Porcupine will make no attempt to back up. Nor will it try to turn around to bite you with its four incisors, which normally would be quite capable of cutting a human finger in two with one bite. Instead, the Porcupine will attempt to drag itself away in the opposite direction. So with the tail immobilised you can reach underneath the body where there are no quills, lift it off the ground and carry it away without injury to either you or the Porcupine.

I must tell you that this procedure applies to the American Porcupine. It has, to my knowledge, never been tried on an African specimen. Don't.

A Porcupine quill is valued as a talisman by Ugandan school children to ensure that they pass their examinations, whilst ceramists assure me that their pliability and strength make them desirable as potters' tools.

The quills themselves are not poisonous and rarely carry an infection into the wound they make. The southern African Porcupine quills have polished points, whilst the American tips are covered with thousands of minute barbs, making them impossible to extract once they have pierced the skin. They neither soften nor dissolve. Each quill must be removed immediately or it will work in deeper and deeper. Dr Albert Shadle, a Porcupine expert at the University of Buffalo, once accidentally had a single quill driven deep into his forearm. He let it stay there and within two days was able to remove it from the opposite side. It had passed completely through his arm and soon dropped free, leaving scarcely a scar.

The hedgehog is also a valuable find, though not financially so. The skin with its bristles was used by Zulu soldiers as a talisman against accidents and to repel the

weapons of the enemy during warfare. The skin was cut into circular pieces, about the size of a large coin, sown onto a leather thong and worn as a headband, the piece of hedgehog skin being placed against the forehead – bristles out, no doubt.

In Morocco the pounded and roasted liver of the hedgehog is given to school boys to make them remember their lessons, whilst in England in the seventeenth century the left eye of the hedgehog fried in oil was a remedy for insomnia.

Talking of insomnia, I was lying in bed one night, thinking, amongst other things, that our road needed some improvements and repairs. At about eleven o'clock the dogs started barking.

'It's the porcupine,' I said, and went back to my thoughts.

But Harry sensed something bigger and bravely went outside armed with a torch and a blunt instrument. What greeted his eyes was a close encounter straight from one of Steven Spielberg's fantasies. Etched against a black sky was a double row of green lights, as tall as a two-storey house. Below, four headlights pierced the darkness and picked out my husband in his pyjamas. It was a double-deckered, treble-trailered Stuttafords Van Lines pantechnicon which had taken a turn for the worse.

It was now perched precariously on the edge of a precipice and my seedlings.

When we had prised his white knuckles from the steering wheel, we persuaded E.T. to phone home and explain his predicament.

The following morning the local towing company was summoned to extract the vehicle from our mountain, to manoeuvre the components so that they went down the road in the proper order. This meant separating the cab from the trailers, turning it round, hoisting the one out of the way while the other was winched to safety. Forty-seven cups of coffee and one wrecked garden later, we waved goodbye to a relieved driver.

The hazards of living in the country, as we have seen, can sometimes come from unexpected quarters, and it would be wise to study the ways of wild things before embarking on anything like an elaborate outdoors wedding.

City friends of ours who 'have a farm in Africa' decided that their only son and heir would have a reception to remember. They chose May (when it never rains); they chose to have the ceremony by the river under the trees (because it's pretty); and they chose to free fancy white pigeons from a cage (to symbolise Peace, Purity and Freedom).

Mistakes.

Guests in their finery came from far and wide, a string quartet played to the sound of distant thunder, and the local choir sang to the wind in the bushwillows. In May the only tree with any canopy of note under which to exchange vows was the African Flame tree, *Spathodia campanulata*, which is host to a certain kind of caterpillar, the name of which escapes me.

The ceremony was long. The caterpillars fell in their thousands, gathered in the wide-brimmed hats, on the padded shoulders, on the white satin gown. Everyone pretended not to notice. The sound of thunder grew louder. The ceremony was long. The time came to set the symbolic pigeons free. When one of the bridesmaids opened the little cage door, the birds didn't notice or care. They were too busy copulating. Everyone pretended not to notice. In the end the bridegroom had to reach in, grab one by the tail and hurl it into the sky. The other one followed. Then the heavens opened up and it poured with rain.

Everyone noticed.

chapter three

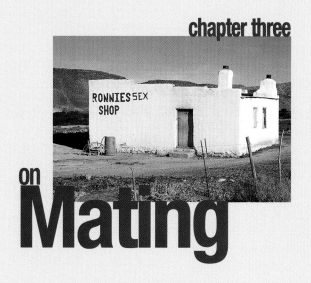

on
Mating

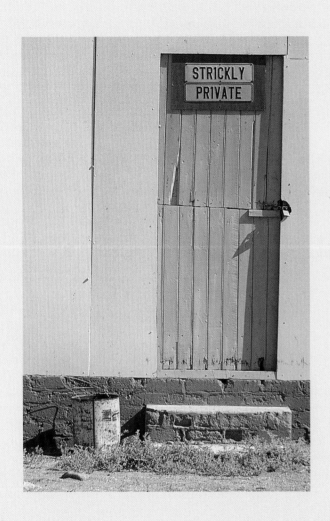

There is no justice in nature. Consider the praying mantis. A hypocrite or, at best, ill named. The word 'mantis' comes from the Greek word meaning prophet or soothsayer, which is descriptive of its posture, holding its front feet as though in devout prayer. But its behaviour is reactionary. The female has a nasty cannibalistic tendency at those times when she should be most polite. Sex may be enjoyable, but for the smaller unfortunate male it's a hazardous business. Pheromones (which provide for sexual attraction), being what they are, send the male into a frenzy, a collision course with disaster. Mindful of his possible fate, he approaches the female warily from behind. Thoughtful Mother Nature has given him a sporting chance by diminishing the female's eyesight. She is, in a word, myopic. She can only see him when he moves. He, however, has excellent vision. So if she turns around and spots him coming, he freezes and can stay motionless until she loses interest. Then steadily he proceeds with caution, until he is finally close enough to leap upon her back and copulate, skilfully dodging his mate's attempts to chew off his head. So absorbed can he become in the task of perpetuating his species that he loses all thought of self-preservation. If perchance she is too quick for him and succeeds in her murderous intentions, his now headless body will continue with the task in hand. Duty done, energy replete, what remains of him slips to the ground and dies. If she's still hungry she may finish him off. Now that's unsociable behaviour for you.

But they do make pretty babies.

The praying mantis, like other insects, has its organs in strange places. Most insects carry their ears on their legs, but in the case of the mantis the ear, or auditory organ, is a membrane in the middle of its thorax, which vibrates in response to high-frequency sounds. Ultrasonic sonar signals sent out by insect-eating bats (inaudible to humans) are detected by the mantis. So what looks to us like inept navigation is the praying mantis deploying evasive tactics in its flight path. Loaded with superstitious connotations, the mantis is also called the pot carrier or Hottentot God. The Turks and Arabs believe that it is in constant supplication to Allah, with its face usually turned towards the holy city of Mecca. Herd-boys in parts of Africa will implore a mantis to point out the direction of a lost beast, but to see a

Praying mantid nymph
(Pseudocreobotra wahlbergi)

mantis swaying from side to side is an evil portent that brings a state of deepest depression to the observer.

My sadistic side (or was it curiosity?) came to the fore when I threw a small green mantis onto a *Nephila's* sticky silk web. The mantis stuck and wriggled and alerted *Nephila*, who immediately left the centre of her web and ran nimbly along a golden radial thread to the ensnared prey. The plucky little mantis reared up and fought all the way but the spider inflicted a fatal bite and the poison instantly started to dissolve the poor fellow's innards. *Nephila* began to wrap the mantis with silk and transport her back to the centre of the web. Meanwhile, at the far end of the web, the male had been watching all this activity with more than just a passing interest. He made his way purposefully towards the boudoir pantry in the hope that he might get a slice of mantis or a chance to mate with his otherwise occupied spouse. He approached with caution, testing the response of the female by stroking one of her back legs with one of his front legs. She didn't seem to notice. She was intent on her task of wrapping up the dinner. So he imprudently lunged forward. His mistake. In no time at all she had him all wrapped up too. Her two food parcels would see her nicely through the next few hours.

The Solifuge is the 'fugitive from the sun', a misnomer indeed, for the Solifuge is most often seen wandering around *in* the sun. Its Afrikaans name, *haarskeerder* (hair cutter) or *baardskeerder* (beard trimmer), comes from the belief that it can become entangled in a woman's hair. It is generally called a hunting spider or a sun spider or even a Roman spider, but is in fact not a spider at all. Its body measures up to 5 cm in length, with a huge hairy head, fierce pointed jaws and two protruding black eyes too close together. It looks as if it's got ten legs but the two in front are pedipalps, which have sucker-like pads at the ends enabling them to scuttle up perpendicular surfaces with no difficulty and great speed. It is also called a Jerrymuglum, or Jerrymander, so called by the soldiers stationed in Egypt during World War One, although I cannot find out why, except that it could have something to do with his scandalous sexual behaviour.

The Solifuge should really be renamed the Subterfuge because, apart from being a fraud spider, it lurks, and lurkers must devise devious means of getting what they

Solifuge

want. Not being true spiders they don't know how to spin a web, so they can snare neither their prey nor a mate. They make up for the former by being ferocious fighters and for the latter by being cads. Crude cads at that. The male Solifuge hurls himself at the female, knocking her senseless, and while she lies motionless on her back, he ejaculates all over the floor, opens her genital orifice with his jaws, scoops up his sperm with his pedipalp and pushes it inside her. She comes to her senses immediately, realises what's hit her and proceeds with the laborious task of excavating a burrow to lay the now fertilised eggs, which *she*, of course, has to care for. Jerrymuglum's nowhere to be seen, *he's* gone a-hunting.

The most hated insect in my house is the fishmoth, which, by the way, is neither a fish nor a moth, so let's call it *Ctenolepisma longicaudata*. It was introduced to South Africa at the turn of the century in the luggage of those pioneering Europeans who brought with them their cargoes of books. As an artist whose stock of paper is guzzled by these nocturnal omnivores, I am further put off by their mating habits. During an elaborate 'dance' the male deposits his spermatophore on the ground in front of the female, who picks it up and squeezes it into her genital aperture. I welcome the spiders that hide in the bookshelves and eat the fishmoths who would otherwise live out their expected life span of five book-eating years.

For the bedbug, mating is a risky business, sometimes tantamount to murder. The male's sexual organ resembles the sharp curved blade of a scimitar. He does not insert it into the female's genital opening but treacherously stabs her in the back and releases the sperm into the bloodstream, which carries it to the reproductive organs. Sometimes the male may actually kill the female; but as a rule, her wounds heal. By counting the number of scars on the back of a female bedbug, we can tell how often she has mated. Even males have scars on their backs, for the bedbugs are unable to distinguish between males and females, and often a male will 'mate' with another male. The male bedbug will stab anything that is (a) the size of a bedbug, (b) dark in colour, and (c) flat in shape.

Snakes have elaborate courtship procedures as well. They have sensitive forked tongues which pick up the scent left behind by the females. A male will approach the female, flicking his tongue over her body. Actual mating takes hours or even days, the

Thick-tailed Bushbaby

pair remaining intertwined until conception is achieved. One would think that having no legs or arms with which to grip each other, they might slip apart; however, when the male's penis is erect it bristles with barbs and becomes firmly anchored within the female, and there they will lie, side by side, for hours. If the female, uninterested in what is happening, decides to wander off, she drags the smaller and now helpless male along with her. If they encounter an enemy and have to part, the penis simply breaks off and he is free to leave. This is not as serious as it seems: Mother Nature thoughtfully provided him with two.

We should not frown upon the mantis's cannibalistic habits, nor the rape of the bedbug and the Solifuge: there is worse to come. The behaviour of the Thick-tailed Bushbaby, *Otolemur crassicaudatus*, takes the cake.

On one of those glorious hot humid nights when I chose to sleep outside on the roof close to the branches of the Acacia tree, out of the way of snakes and scorpions, I was awakened by the feeling that I was not alone. It was full moon, so I could see the bushbaby clearly. He sat on a branch not three metres from me, silent and unaware of my presence. His hand and foot on one side of the body were raised simultaneously, then passed under the genital region where his hand was urinated upon.

He then grasped his foot a couple of times with his hand, smearing the urine onto it. This action was then repeated on the other side, while he gazed fixedly into the distance rhythmically swaying his head and body.

Sometimes in the dead of night we hear the eerie shriek of this strange canopy-dwelling animal, sounding like a cry for help from a desperate potential murder victim. Now I only think of him as a tortured soul having to perform disgusting rituals in the belief that it will make him more attractive to a mate. Perhaps it does. Certain Tswana tribes burn pangolins in their kraals in the belief that this will enhance the fertility of their stock. Its scales are collected for decorations and other ritual purposes with the result that it is now on the Endangered Species list.

If a man is on the prowl for a ladylove, in Zulu culture, the Orange-throated Longclaw is the bird to see to bring him good luck on his quest. It also has the added significance in folklore as the robin and crossbill in Europe and America. When there was no one to wipe the blood from the face of our Lord on the Cross, this bird came and rubbed its neck on His face till the blood stopped. When it saw His face no longer bleeding, it retired, receiving its legacy – the blood mark on its neck.

In an abandoned termite mound near the old marula tree lives, from time to time, a family of Dwarf Mongooses. They are led by a matriarch who chooses her mate, and only this pair is allowed to rear young. The dominant male leads the group into battle, teaches the young how to forage, is the only one who mates with the matriarch female and has the job of preventing illicit sex amongst the rest of the group, most of which are his offspring anyway. Anne Rasa in her study entitled *Mongoose Watch* says that the male Dwarf Mongoose mounted his mate Diane 2386 times, which is not only an astounding feat in itself but a telling test of observer patience.

Near my studio grows an old *stamvrug* tree, *Englerophytum magaliesmontanum*. It supports lichens, mosses, clumps of orchids and a fine crop of Jew's Ears. The name Jew's Ear is due to a mistranslation of its Latin name, *Auricularia auricula judae* or Judas' ear. According to legend, the fungus grew on the elder tree from which Judas Iscariot hanged himself. Although it is not the most appetising of fungi to look at, it has a good flavour. It is also used as a poultice for inflamed eyes and as a gargle for inflammation of the throat.

But if you are seeking a remedy for a problem of a different kind, it is to the clumps of orchids that you must turn your attention. The word 'orchis' is Greek and means testicles. Legend has it that Orchis was the lascivious son of Patellanus, a satyr, and the nymph Acolasia. Orchis went to a festival given by Bacchus, where, imbibing too much

Dwarf Mongoose preening

Lions mating

of the grape and being therefore lustful, he seduced one of the priestesses. The people were so angry that they tore his body into many pieces and threw them into the air. Patellanus, his father, pleaded with the gods to reassemble his son and restore him to life, but they insisted that Orchis deserved his fate for leading such a lecherous life, conceding that flowers should be allowed to grow wherever little bits of Orchis lay scattered.

The bulbous roots of *Lissochilus arenius* are said by the Zulus to be the most powerful means of overcoming barrenness in women and serve a man well in acts of love.

The stems of the Leopard Orchid, *Ansellia gigantea*, are also used as aphrodisiacs. A Zulu man will place a small bit of the leaf under his arm ornaments as a talisman to aid him in his courtship. Used as an infusion it is said to expel bad dreams, whereas inhaling a smouldering root will expurgate madness. On the other hand, *Ansellia humilis*, being ever so humble, is made into a leaf infusion but instead of promoting sexual activity, it is said to render a maiden barren.

The orchid family has two main branches: those whose flowers have one tail and those with two tails. The flowers of the genus *Satyrium* have two long tails at the rear of the flower, suggestive of those Greek woodland gods, called satyrs, with horses' ears and tails and sometimes the budding horns of goats.

Gazing at *Satyrium erectum* in September 1774, the botanist Carl Thunberg noted that the hooded yellow flowers with their long spurs suggested the Cape sun bonnet and gave the plant the name *geelkappie*. He seems to have missed the point.

A rather uninspiring orchid whose tubers are burned and the resultant ash rubbed into incisions is said to cure ailing limbs. It is *Eulophia flaccida*, an infusion of which is also given to women until they conceive. With a name like that it's obvious that their potency rests more in the female than the male.

Talking of orchids and misguided behaviour, there's a beetle, *Peritrichia*, which burrows into the ground during winter and falls asleep. In spring the male beetle emerges a few weeks before the female. In the same area lives an orchid called *Orthopenthea fasciata* which gives off a pheromone identical to the sex attractant of the female beetle. Not only that but the orchid has evolved a configuration of its petals almost identical to that of this particular female in a receptive sexual posture. So while the female is still sleeping, the male beetle, being not a little myopic, is attracted by the smell of the

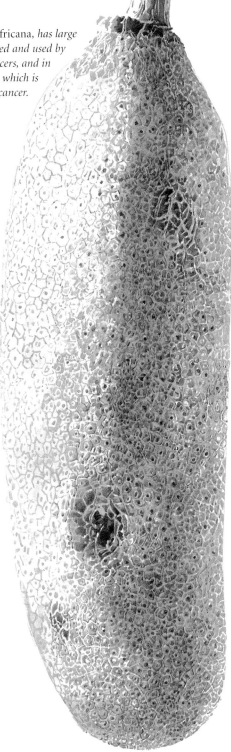

The Sausage tree, Kigelia africana, *has large pendulous fruits that are crushed and used by the Tsonga as dressings for ulcers, and in Zimbabwe a skin cream is made which is effective in the treatment of skin cancer.*

orchid and, it being springtime, performs his duty accordingly and the orchids are effectively cross-pollinated. When the females wake up and exude the same pheromones the beetles are all of a tither and have to make amends. The fact that they are not extinct proves that they have ample reserves and inclination.

In Louisiana it is said that if you fall out of a fig tree you'll never get well; also that if fig trees are planted on land which has not been paid for, the land will never be paid for.

In parts of Africa and in Italy, the fig tree is the spiritual husband of barren women. The fig leaves worn by Adam and Eve to cover their nakedness were used because they were the largest leaves growing in Palestine. A puny olive leaf, which is the symbol of peace, would hardly have served the purpose.

It is astonishing, when you really go into it, just how many mythological creatures there are to scare the hell out of us. There's the leprechaun, the goblin, the poltergeist, bogeyman and doppelgänger, banshees and kelpies, ogres and trolls, gremlins, elves and jinn, but none can be as diabolical as the Tokoloshe of Africa.

Traditionally, Tokoloshe was a harmless but mischievous character who constantly played tricks on people; however, he becomes harmful when he is caught by a witch.

'He is described as having an exceedingly large male member, which, due to its size, has to be carried over the shoulders and around the neck. He is "hairy, like a pig," of short stature, and because of the very frequent intercourse in which Tokoloshe indulges, his right hip and buttock are said to have worn away.'

I decline to draw him.

~

Shane tells me that bananas are extraordinary. If you have a bowl of bananas in the same room as a vase of flowers, especially carnations, then the flowers will wilt and die very quickly. He tells me it's the toxic chemical, ethylene, that they give off.

Axel-Ivar Berglund confirms their peculiarity by noting that amongst the Zulus bananas have a significant symbolism. 'They distinguish bananas from other fruit in that banana plants become pregnant (*ukumitha*) when carrying fruit, whereas other trees *khahlela* or *twala*, carry. Fruit trees in general are said to have *izithelo* (fruit), but bananas have *amazinyane* (literally, offspring), related to living species.'

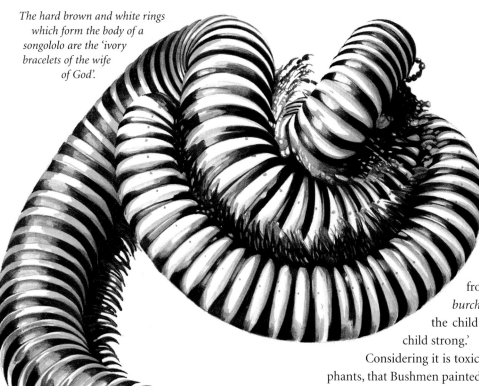

Bananas are identified with men, and pregnant women avoid eating them; however, they are readily eaten by women who wish to become pregnant but do not conceive.

Red, the colour of blood and frequently related to menstruation and pregnancy as a symbol, plays an important role in fertility and pregnancy.

Expectant women were given medicines prepared from the large red roots of *intolwane, Elephantorrhiza burchelli* (elephantina). 'This medicine is like blood. It makes the child strong. Even the bitterness of the medicine makes the child strong.'

Considering it is toxic to sheep, dangerous to eland, barely manageable to elephants, that Bushmen painted with the pigment, Boers roasted the dried seeds for coffee, and the roots were used for tanning and dyeing leather, it is hardly surprising that it is capable of providing resistance against all the difficulties life has to offer a delicate unborn human baby whose mother nibbled on its root.

'If a woman does not conceive although she had regular menstruations, the red root of *isinama esibomvu sehlathi* (*Pupalia atropurpurea*) is pounded and prepared into a paste. Of this paste two balls, "like a man" (i.e. testicles), are prepared. One is eaten by the husband and the other inserted into the vagina by the woman prior to intercourse. That night the blood mixes nicely. She will conceive of the medicine.'

~

It seems as if it's not much better to be a male if you're a reptile. Although the male lizard still has to put in quite a bit of effort to catch her, the female is not particularly willing, and has to be immobilised with a sharp bite on the nape of the neck.

This morning I found a black and white striped songololo and wanted to paint him. I put him into a deep glass bowl and went to the compost heap to get a spadeful of compost for his comfort and my background. On the way I

At Christmas time in the southern hemisphere, and over Lulu Phezulu in particular, there is sometimes a blizzard of white butterflies flurrying across the veld, headed east. They are Catopsilia florella (African Vagrant or Cabbage White), the larvae of which can devastate large areas of leguminous cassia plants.

picked up another songololo. I put him in the bowl too. Instantly they bound themselves together, their jaws stuck into each other's soft under-throats, locked in mortal combat. Two males in a confined space in the breeding season fight to the death. I had great difficulty in separating them, their combined 200 legs clinging tight.

It is said that if you step on a millipede and squash him, you will laugh uncontrollably for a hundred years.

~

Love has many subtleties and many moods. One moment passionate and aglow with colour and fiery lights and the next moment the full white glow of companionship. Love is as rare as opals and ivory. And as precious.

~

A male toad approaches all moving objects during the breeding season and tries to clasp them. The male releases its grip only if the clasped object gives the defensive call of another male. Females remain silent and continue to be clasped, as are carps, the human hand, old boots and any other silent slimy damp objects.

Stick insects have been known to copulate for 79 days at a stretch.

Males of a certain species of damselfly deploy a specially hooked penis in their fight to father youngsters. They use this instrument to withdraw sperm left inside their mates by rivals, before making their own deposits.

Strange behaviour during courtship is one thing, but for some Acraeid butterflies the mating itself is unusual. The male *Acraea*, having found an available female *Acraea* and while still in flight, will grab her on the back of her thorax. The pair will then tumble from the sky with the female apparently trying to escape from the male. On reaching stable ground the female is held down while the male mates with her. To ensure that he alone will mate with her he plugs the genital opening with a waxy deposit called 'sphragis' (which rhymes with haggis), and then collapses into a comatose state. The next possible suitor will have to check first whether she is a 'plugged' or 'unplugged' female.

Incidentally, the larva or caterpillar of the *Acraea*, like the African Monarch Butterfly, feeds on plants containing chemical compounds which are stored in the

Protogoniomorpha parhassus aethiops
(female) Mother-of-Pearl.

body of the butterfly, making it unpalatable to predators. Some species of *Acraea* feed on *Adenia lobata*, a plant so toxic that it is used for arrow poison.

Sometimes it's just a case of 'you are what you eat'.

'The roots of *ihlamvu lomfana nentombazana* (*Gloriosa virescens*) resemble partly the male organ, partly the female. The symbolism is utilised in various ways. Men, whose wives have given birth to girls and who desire male children, are treated with the root resembling the male, while, if they desire girls, the female root is administered. On the other hand, women who have only girls are treated with roots resembling the female organ while if they have only boys and wish to have a girl, are treated with the root resembling a male.' Axel-Ivar Berglund says he was told that the treatment is also applicable to cattle.

The flame lily,
Gloriosa superba.

C.A. Smith, however, in his *Common Names of South African Plants*, published in 1966, states that '*G. superba* in all its parts contains an acrid narcotic poison and is said to be not infrequently used in India for suicidal purposes, and that *G. virescens* probably contains the same ingredients'. He was probably right because now the taxonomists have changed their minds again, as is their wont, and have decided that they are one and the same plant; all *Gloriosa*s are now called *superba*.

Talking of suicide, the bamboo *Phyllostachys bambusoides* of Sumatra lives to the age of about 120 years, and when the climatic conditions are ideal, it flowers and fruits for the first and last time in one giant suicidal burst of fecundity.

Now the last word on the subject of mating is a little tricky because, the fact is, there isn't one. Surely it was a little remiss of the originators of the English language not to have made up a single polite verb for the one activity around which a great deal of thought, conversation and activity revolves. It is shrouded in euphemisms, alluded to, treated with ribald humour, cloaked in metaphors or given the cumbersome coldness of the term 'indulging in sexual intercourse'.

chapter four

on
Breeding

The spring rains bring with them a reawakening of the vitality of nature. The burgeoning of the bush happens within days and hundreds of birds appear as if from nowhere. The hillsides are tinged with green and the insects buzz, bumble and bite.

Winter was over, the final touches to the house were complete, and so we took a drive to see a waterfall we'd been told about. There are many waterfalls in the surrounding mountains, set in deep narrow gorges, flanked by indigenous forest, thick with mosses, orchids and ferns. After our simple picnic I dozed off while the children went off on their own.

Now the Yellow-banded African Bee, *Apis mellifera adansonii*, is an aggressive, restless, politically unstable individual but, *en masse*, is a tour de force. To see one's small children come hurtling out of a forest covered in bees is an awesome sight. Instinct is strong in all of us, especially in children covered in bees. They both plunged into the icy pool at the base of the waterfall. Motherly instinct sent me straight in after them. We all thrashed about and most of the bees came off but there were still some clinging to hair and clothing and most of the stings were still in the flesh. With hardly a second wasted and dripping wet, I drove at top speed, lights on, hooter blaring, to the nearest hospital. Max was in for three days, Walter for two, yet after a week they were boasting to their friends how many stings they had had. The number grew with each telling.

I harbour no resentment against the honey bee. It provides us with one of nature's finest foods, but the poor thing has a miserable social life. All the workers are sterile females, gathering the food, feeding the larvae, removing the garbage, grooming and cleaning the queen, morning till night, dusk till dawn, seven days a week. A woman's work is never done. But when the queen decrees, she takes to the air, followed by some faithful but unsuspecting male drones, whose only reason for existence is to fertilise the queen and die. She then makes her way back to the colony where her royal subjects pamper her for the rest of her life, while she occupies herself by laying eggs. She is able to determine what sex each newly laid egg will be, thereby assuring the community of an evenly balanced society. Most of them become workers, the proletariat. If the colony needs to expand, the workers augment the diet of some female larvae, causing them to develop into young debutante queens. The old queen begins to lay unfertilised eggs, causing only males to emerge, unaware that they have been created solely for expedient exploitation – to mate with those chosen females now to be groomed for the Good Life.

Honeybees practised pharmacology long before people. They use propolis, a resin collected from plants and trees, especially poplars, for plugging various spaces in the nest cavity. The substance also has a strong anti-bacterial, microbial and viral activity. This 'bee-glue' is apparently also a traditional human remedy used in East European folk medicine, but I know it as the resin used for varnishing Stradivarius violins.

Having ridiculously large feet and leading an existence that can only be described as precarious, walking about on constantly sinking salad, should be enough for any bird to contend with, but the male African Jacana also has an unstable relationship with his mate. The female weighs nearly twice as much as the male and has a dominating demeanour to match. All the available males are monopolised by those females who, with brute force, have both subdued the male of their choice and aggressively dispatched any other competing female. Brawling on waterlily leaves is a risky business, with the losers likely to lose more than just their balance. The successful victress is a prolific egg-layer, sometimes laying up to ten clutches per season, and if they all hatch, that's a lot of precocious precocial lily-trotter chicks. While the female is frantically involved in fending off female competition or casting a roving eye around the pond, the male is saddled with the chicks, which he carries awkwardly under his wings as he wades unsteadily about looking for some-

Jacana

Button-quail

thing to eat; in an emergency, he can take to the air without letting go of the children clinging to his wingpits.

The eggs of the jacana look as if they have been decorated by Kandinsky and then given a glossy coat of french polish. Choice spots, such as idyllic pools garnished with waterlilies and seasoned with aquatic delicacies, attract predatory egg-eaters such as Water Mongooses, leguaans, otters and snakes. Eggs that are not stolen fall off or through the nests, which are nothing more than 'careless accumulations of waterlily stems and soggy sticks, vulnerable to the elements, the flooding vlei and the receding river'.

There is a nasty word for the behaviour of the female button-quail. In most species of birds the males are more attractive than the females. But as we have seen with the jacana, so it is with the button-quail, which is also much larger and more colourful than the cock. Once she has laid her eggs, she goes off amusing herself by fighting other hens and toying with unbuttoned male quails, while her own mate sits dutifully on the nest incubating the eggs and providing food for the chicks.

Female European Bee-eaters, on the other hand, ensure that their mates play an equal role in the task of bringing up the brood. To test their potential, the males are put through their paces. 'While the female watches from a nearby branch, the male catches an insect, and returns to the perch beside her, fanning his tail and calling loudly.' If she decides the gift is suitable she lies almost horizontally across the branch with her feathers ruffled, while the male copulates. This is known as courtship feeding, and probably plays a role in the nutritional well-being of the female. This is certainly the case with the Common Tern: the more food the male brings, the more eggs the female lays.

In the case of eagles, particularly the Black Eagle, both the male and female are model parents, in all but one respect. They do not prevent the one chick from slaugh-

Jacana

The Black Korhaan,
in display, flies up calling
'krak krak krraka krraka
kraka kraka', cruises around,
then slowly descends with
rapidly flapping wings, dangling
his yellow legs.

Stanley's Bustard

tering the other. Known as the Cain and Abel syndrome, or obligate siblicide, the stronger of the two chicks kicks and pecks its sibling to death, thus ensuring the undivided attention of its devoted parents.

The bustards are the macho men of the avian world. Unlike the dutiful Black Eagle parents, the male bustard, after a brief copulation, leaves the female to incubate the eggs and rear the chicks on her own. He may weigh up to twice as much as the female. He is, without exception, more impressive, having developed remarkable display plumage and behaviour calls to attract as many females as possible.

The Kori Bustard, the largest of the bustards, has a deep booming call and, when displaying, the male inflates his neck, raises his tail over his back and spreads out the fluffy feathers under his tail in an enticing fan.

The Red-crested Korhaan has a spectacular display. He flies vertically up to about twenty metres and then 'stalls', fluffs out his feathers and free-falls to earth, pulling up and gliding away to land safely at the last minute. Normally the red crest is hidden but, when excited in the presence of a female, a crest of little red feathers sticks out on the nape of the neck.

Its call has, more than once, caused me to pull over and check the car for a mechanical fault. A dozen or so loud clicks sound like a loose axle-bearing. Then, when the call becomes an even louder piping call, it sounds as if the wheel is actually falling off.

Both the Black and the Black-bellied Korhaans have flight displays that are quite absurd. The male Black-bellied Korhaan flies for 'several metres with slow exaggerated wingbeats, showing conspicuous white wings, then glides to the ground with the wings held up at an angle above the horizontal, neck extended and raised, the feet drawn up and the black chest puffed out'.

If you are travelling in the eastern parts of the country, you can be certain it's the Black-bellied Korhaan you're watching, but in the dry west it's always the Black Korhaan. Ne'er the twain shall meet. Similarly, the Pale and the Dark Chanting Goshawks' territories never cross, the Pale occurring only in the dry desert areas, and the Dark only in the east.

The Stanley's Bustard, when displaying, elongates his white neck, ruffling his long chest feathers. If he is perched on a conspicuous site he can be seen from up to three kilometres away.

The Red-billed Hoopoe, the White-browed Sparrow Weaver and the Helmet-shrikes are all matriarchal. Only one female of the flock lays eggs and the young chicks are fed by all the aunts and older chicks of a previous brood.

With a few unfortunate exceptions Mother Nature deals severely with prolific breeders. Guppies, those tiny aquarian fish that we all kept as children, were the subject of an experiment by two scientists, Breder and Coates. Two tanks of equal size, each with an abundant food supply, were placed side by side. Into one of the tanks the scientists put fifty guppies with an unnatural distribution of one-third males, one-third females and one-third juveniles. In the other tank they placed a single female, heavy with fertilised eggs.

Over a period of six weeks the lone female produced three broods of twenty-five each, yet at the end of that time there remained only nine fish in her tank. She had eaten the surplus young. Meanwhile, in the other tank there had been a catastrophe. Total infanticide had befallen the newborn and the adults were down to nine in number. In each tank there were now three males and six females, the ordained proportion amongst guppies.

One of my failings is that I am human, and have compassion. If I had been a guppy things might have been different.

On one of those moonless nights, in the middle of winter, I was in a deep sleep when I was awakened by a violent knocking on the back door. One of the builders' wives was in labour. I ran to the kraal and groped my way through the darkened door-way, alarmed to find half a dozen faces looking at me eerily illuminated by the flame of a single candle. On the bed, which was raised on bricks as per custom, was Nora, her legs drawn up, her chest and stomach covered by a blanket. From her groans I knew she was in considerable pain.

I was about to send the audience away when I remembered about the African Spiny Mouse, which occurs in the dry northern parts of the Kruger National Park. She has the curious habit of always giving a breech presentation, assisted by many mousy mid-wives, who all keep a beady eye on the situation.

The Black-bellied Korhaan's call sounds like a cork being slowly drawn from a bottle and popping out.

When the mouse-baby's legs appear the mother bends over and licks them. The midwife mice crowd around. The surrounding membranes tear and are licked away by the First Midwife mouse. The mother mouse lies back and allows the baby mouse to enter the world, bringing the afterbirth with it. This is eaten by the Senior Midwife mouse.

I decided to keep my audience of midwives in case any licking had to be done, and chose to forget about the African Spiny Mouse and concentrate on the matter in hand. Suddenly I saw that Nora had involuntarily started pushing, and two legs stuck out stiff and dark. Wasn't the head supposed to come out first? The people of the Valley of a Thousand Hills say that if a pregnant woman eats standing up, then the baby will come out into the world standing up.

Despite the seriousness of the situation, my mind wandered again to the animal kingdom, and I could not help thinking of a duck, legs and tail in the air looking for food in a dark pond. I then felt suddenly very afraid and alone. The audience was mute and unresponsive. Rolling up my sleeves I ordered a large capable-looking woman to fetch a basin of hot water, clean towels and newspaper. She seemed uninterested, even reluctant, muttering, 'It is no use, it is no use.'

Dark eyes continued to peer at me from all corners of the room, so I asserted my command and dispatched midwife number two with a message for Harry to hasten the ambulance. Resuming my role, I bent over the half-visible baby and gently tried to coax it from the mother's body, at the same time urging Nora to push.

Why can't babies be like eggs? This one was going against the nap.

Suddenly the mother's abdomen heaved and a little purple creature slipped out onto the newspaper. I grabbed it by the feet, turned it upside down and shook it vigorously. I was relieved but scared. It did not respond with the lusty customary cry. The body was limp and still. All the midwives shook their heads and urged me to throw it away. Had there been any more light in the room I probably would have, but couldn't see properly, so I laid it gently down on clean newspaper, wiped its face with a damp cloth and gave mouth-to-mouth respiration. That is, I puffed regular bursts of carbon dioxide into what felt like its face while my fingers massaged the tiny chest. There was still no movement although the heart was beating faintly. I continued for a while until I remembered the afterbirth. Taking hold of the umbilical cord, I pulled gently, pleading with Nora to push. At last an AWFUL THING slid out. I turned my attention again to the baby, which was so small it could be held in the palm of my hand. As I pumped the chest with my fingers the tiny form suddenly jerked its limbs and snorted. Life. One of the midwives snapped out of her stupor and wiped Nora's face. I can't remember what I did with the string and scissors. I scooped up the pile of stuff, which I suppose was the placenta, wrapped it in the bloody, wet newspapers and put it in a bucket. Every few minutes the baby's body went limp again, so I jiggled it about a bit, wishing the ambulance would hurry. The midwives clicked their tongues and shook their heads as they watched me work on the mauve shape.

Suddenly headlights of a vehicle lit up the doorway and the yard was filled with people. No one was concerned about the state of the baby. It had already been dismissed as a thing of the past, a non-starter. The driver was only interested in names, addresses and ambulance fees. I wrapped the baby in a sheet, the icy-cold cord dangling, and handed it to someone in a white coat. Then, I think, I passed out.

The following morning I phoned the hospital, expecting to hear that the baby had been 'dead on arrival', but was told that both mother and son were in a satisfactory condition. The baby was in an incubator and was doing as well as could be expected, weighing in at two pounds ten ounces. I phoned every day for nine days. On the tenth day, baby Alfred died.

～

In the case of turtles only two per cent make it to adulthood. Only twenty per cent of the lion cubs in the Kalahari Gemsbok Park survive. The weakest die of mange or other diseases; the inept are killed while learning to catch and kill Gemsbok; and the unfit starve. The ecology of the desert is fragile, capable of supporting only a certain number of each species, be it lion or butterfly.

All areas on this planet are vulnerable to a greater or lesser degree. Although one should not advocate marching like lemmings to the nearest ocean, marching has become fashionable these days, so one might pause in one's protest against the cause of the moment to wonder why.

Nature has devised a scale of proliferation for each of her species and an effective method of controlling its growth. Just open a jar of Lumpfish caviar to find out how plentiful could have been the Sturgeon. The lemmings know what to do when the time is right. As humans we may have side-stepped or foolishly outwitted Nature's plan.

As mothers, being loved by our children gives us a false sense of worth, because even the most neglectful, selfish, theoretically worthless women are loved by their children, and we go on breeding, breeding.

If you look carefully, you may notice that this chapter is quite short. It's because I'm embarrassed about the proliferation of my own family. From a quickie in the spring of 1670 a gigantic broccoli took root and thrived, spreading its seed and florets far and wide. As a methodical genealogist I have been meticulous in documenting each cousin. Surely it's time someone *did* something about it? I don't know *who* and I don't know *what*, but I do know *why*.

We're as common as Lumpfish caviar.

Detail from the Jeppe family tree
1670–1994

on
Naming

T AXONOMISTS CONNIVE to confuse the student of nature. If they are not busy changing the names, they offer misleading ones.

The Brown Snake Eagle is *Circaetus cinereus*, Latin for grey.

The Black-backed Cisticola is *Cisticola galactotes*, Greek for milk-white.

The Latin name for the White-breasted Cormorant is *Phalacrocorax carbo*, which means black, as in carbon.

The Yellow-breasted Pipit is *Anthus chloris*, which is Latin for green.

For the Spotted Flycatcher, it is *Muscicapa striata*, which, of course, means striped.

The Black Cuckooshrike is called *Campephaga flava*, which means yellow.

The Brown-hooded Kingfisher is called *Halcyon albiventris*, which means 'white below'.

The Black-shouldered Kite is called *Elanus caeruleus*, which means blue.

The White-fronted Bee-eater has the reddest of red fronts, and the Black-collared Barbet is recognised more by its red face than its black collar.

The Golden-breasted Bunting, with its vivid yellow breast, is called in Afrikaans *Rooirugstreepkoppie*, which literally translates as Redbackedstripedhead, thus consciously avoiding its most diagnostic feature.

Then there's the White-headed Black-headed Canary (which should perhaps have been Striped-headed Canary?).

The Yelloweyed Canary does not have a yellow eye.

A Cattle Egret, or 'tick-bird' as it is often called, does not really eat ticks. It is usually seen around herds of grazing cattle, sheep or antelope, feeding on the grasshoppers, bugs and beetles that the animals flush out as they move through the grass.

And anyone who has seen the sun catching the back of the male Plum-coloured Starling can be forgiven for being puzzled by its being called *Cinnyricinclus leucogaster* – white belly.

The plain, boring Blue Crane is embellished with the name *Anthropoides paradisea*,

whilst its sister, the flamboyant Crowned Crane, is simply called *Balearica regulorum.*

The world's finest table grape – the largest and the sweetest, the Hanepoot – does not bear any resemblance to a cock's foot; the word was a euphemism and should be *hanekloot*, which means testicle.

Spanish Moss is not a moss, it's a lichen.

A rose is a rose is a rose is a rose but the Marsh Rose is not a rose, it's a protea, *Orothamnus zeyheri*; nor is the desert rose, it's a rock.

Tomb bats don't live in tombs but in open savanna woodland.

Cassia abbreviata has a pod as long as your arm.

Ringworms are not worms, they are fungi (species of the mould *Trichophyton*).

A fishmoth is neither a fish nor a moth.

Bombay duck is not a duck, but a Chinese fish dish.

Now the Egyptian Goose, *Alopochen aegyptiacus*, which, as we all know, laid the Celestial Egg from which the world originated, is in fact not a goose but a duck. The fact that our origins are from duck eggs puts a better perspective on things.

The Spurwinged Goose, *Plectropterus gambensis*, is also not a goose, but a duck;

the same with the Pygmy Goose, *Nettapus auritus*.

And as for the mongoose . . .

I derive a great deal of pleasure dabbling in etymology, so when I came across three birds with similar specific names sourcing from the word 'supercilious', I looked up the definition of the word. *Supercilious (adj.) assuming an air of contemptuous indifference or superiority.*

The Olive Bee-eater (*Merops superciliosus*), the Yellow-throated Sparrow (*Petronia superciliaris*) and the White-browed Coucal (*Centropus superciliosus loandae*) – all these birds do not have 'attitude', they simply have white eyebrows. *Superciliary (adj.) of or concerning the eyebrow; over the eye.* A simple diagnostic observation.

Then they run out of names.

The majestic Sable antelope shares a name with a little weasel-like creature of the northern hemisphere.

The Uganda Cob is an antelope as well as a fish.

A yak is not only a long-haired Tibetan ox, it's also a duck found on the Amazon River.

The word 'ostrich' is derived from the Greek word meaning 'sparrow'.

~

Botanical taxonomists are orderly folk striving to create international conformity and consensus. Common names for plants are confusing; for instance, there are many different species of *Homeria* and *Moraea*, all called 'tulp'. The description might be accurate enough for a certain area but the species would differ drastically from place to place. Latin names are most often and very conveniently a description of a diagnostic feature of the plant itself, such as *splendida, deliciosus, elegans, horridus.*

If you're walking through long yellow grass, beware, for you may be walking through buffalo grass, which has the descriptive name of how you would react if confronted by one. The Latin name for buffalo grass is *Panicum maximum.*

Sometimes a plant is named after a place, in which case 'ensis', as in *capensis* is added; or 'ana', as in *africana.*

When a plant is named after a person, the gender of the person is indicated by the suffix of the species name. If the person was female then 'ae' is affixed, as in *Aloe lettyae* (after Cythna Letty) and *Strumeria barbariae* (after my mom!). Perhaps the fact that a woman's surname may change more than once during her lifetime has something to do with it.

If the person was a male, then 'ii' or 'i' is used, as in *Aloe marlothii* or *Combretum zeyheri.* However, the taxonomists could not bring themselves to accord the person fully the honour they deserve – the names are never written with a respectful capital letter.

Early taxonomists, explorers, collectors and dealers in museum specimens were colourful characters.

It is considered bad form to name a discovery after yourself, you have to wait to be so honoured. 'But Adolphe Delegorgue saw no reason for such modesty. He visited South Africa on a hunting trip around 1839, and when he published an account of his

Wilf, our ex next-door-neighbour-across-the-river, has a favourite descriptive species name: Ptenopus garulus garulus, *the barking gecko.*

Temminck's Courser

travels he described two new species, and affixed his name to them' – viz. the Harlequin Quail, *Coturnix delegorguei*, and Delegorgue's Pigeon, *Columba delegorguei*.

Poor Johan August Wahlberg, far from his native Sweden, collected over two thousand bird skins, many reptiles, amphibians and pressed plants during his travels in southern Africa, but at the age of forty-six he was trampled to death by a wounded elephant in northern Botswana. Yet all he got named after him was a rather boring brown bird (*Aquila wahlbergi*); a butterfly which mimics another (*Hypolimnas anthedon wahlbergi*); a pale moth (*Imbrasia wahlbergia*); a frog (*Arthroleptis wahlbergi*); a gecko (*Homopholis wahlbergi*); a few rather uninspiring plants, *Eutada wahlbergii* and *Euphorbia wahlbergii*; and a bat, albeit an epauletted one (*Epomophorus wahlbergi*).

Coenraad Jacob Temminck (1778–1858) founded the collection of birds at the Rijksmuseum in Leiden and was its director for forty years. He also had his own private collection of birds, both stuffed and in aviaries, and in later years he hoarded rare specimens, which he jealously locked away from other ornithologists. He had a courser named after him, whose behaviour could be reminiscent of his own body language on seeing another ornithologist approaching. Roberts states that the Temminck's Courser 'when alarmed raises and lowers its body by straightening and bending its legs, keeping its legs still'.

The characteristics of a Pangolin, that skulking, hole-dwelling, nocturnal rodent that curls up when confronted, further mirrors the behaviour of our curious Mr Temminck. Is it coincidence that the Pangolin, too, is named after him – *Manis temminckii?*

Wilhelm Peter Eduard Simon Rüppell (1794–1884) was born in Germany, the son of a wealthy banker. He collected and described many species from Sinai, Egypt and Abyssinia. His books and maps brought him fame and he was the first foreigner to be awarded a gold medal by the Royal Geographical Society. On his travels he suffered many hardships but returned to Europe with not inconsiderable collections of zoological material, to the Museum of the Natural History Society in Frankfurt, where he undertook the task of cataloguing them. However, as a result of failing health and an inability to work with other museum staff, this task was never completed and 'he ended his life as a crotchety old bachelor living off a meagre pension, his expeditions having exhausted all his own funds'. Of all the parrots Rüppell's Parrot (*Poicephalus rueppellii*) is the dowdiest, of all the korhaans Rüppell's Korhaan (*Eupodotis rueppellii*) is the dullest, and of all the vultures Rüppell's Vulture (*Gryps rueppellii*) is quite the ugliest.

Pangolin

In contrast, François le Vaillant, born in Dutch Guiana in 1753 of French parents, was a flamboyant, controversial explorer who travelled in South Africa from 1781 to 1784. He eloped, aged 23, fathered two children and set off five years later for the Cape on board the ship *Held Woltemade*. His name was actually Vaillant, which means 'valiant', but he changed it to Le Vaillant – 'The Valiant' – which, he felt, sounded more imposing. He had a pet baboon, named Kees, which was his 'faithful travelling companion'. About Kees he said, 'If any crime was committed to which gluttony was the incentive, if any theft of eatables was discovered, Kees was instantly accused, and the accusation was seldom unfounded', and 'An ape … is lascivious, gluttonous, thievish, revengeful and passionate; and if he has not the vice of lying, the savages say it is because he does not choose to talk.'

On his return to France he published a set of magnificently illustrated volumes, *Histoire naturelle des Oiseaux d'Afrique* (1790–1808). Some of the birds and animals included are, in fact, not from Africa at all and others are figments of his vivid imagination. Despite his leanings towards the creative, his name was given to several South African species and he himself named many, such as the Bateleur, Klaas's Cuckoo (after his faithful Khoi servant) and the aforementioned Narina Trogon.

Perhaps these early explorers and collectors should have been taken to task for their avaricious hunting forays. Le Vaillant once boasted that the glossy starlings were so numerous around the Gamtoos River that he killed 80 with five or six shots.

Thomas Ayres was a collector living in 1865 in Potchefstroom where he collected thousands of birds, beetles, butterflies and moths. At least sixty species are now very rare in the area or no longer occur there at all.

Julie, one of the most faithful and intelligent of the Khoi women who accompanied

Burchell throughout his four-year expedition, is commemorated in the name *Anisodontea julii*, the only known instance of a plant named after an indigenous African. Poor Julie, for the shrubby little plant was used in the making of brooms for sweeping the yard.

A 'Comic' Tern is not what you think it is. Because of the difficulty in separating the Common and Arctic Terns in the field, ornithologists have opted for joining the two names together, and they use the same name for both.

As I live in a summer rainfall area, the letter *r* in the name of the month tells me that the rain should be falling or that the roaring of the sands at Witsand can be heard. It also tells me it's safe to eat oysters.

Now if you thought that a frog was a frog was a frog was a frog, besides being the unjustifiable derogatory word for a Frenchman, it's also a hollow in the top face of a brick for holding the mortar; the nut of a violin bow; an elastic horny substance in the sole of a horse's foot; an ornamental coat-fastening of a spindle-shaped button and loop; an attachment to a waist-belt to support a sword or bayonet; and, finally, a grooved piece of iron at a place in a railway where tracks cross.

The frog was, not so long ago, more numerous than any other land vertebrate. It does not turn into a prince, nor does it give you warts, but within its ranks exists the most poisonous creature on earth, the diminutive *Dendrobates pumilio*. 'When a frog is suspended over a fire by Indians of Central America it exudes droplets of poison enough to cover 50 arrow tips. The poison is known as Tetrodotoxin, and 1/3000 grain will quickly kill a man if introduced through a wound in the skin. There is no known antidote.'

There are, you'll be pleased to note, no seriously poisonous frogs in South Africa.

Bateleur

~

There is a saying, 'he is as obstinate as a toad'. We have friends in the valley with whom we occasionally have supper. On balmy nights the table is usually set in their fern-filled atrium which boasts a lily-pond. In spring, due to the raucous serenading of the male frogs, human conversation is impossible. All the guests take turns catching the frogs and depositing them on the lawn in the garden, whereupon they immediately turn around and proceed back to the pond and start up again. Dennis tried to build a little wooden barrier across the doorway but the frogs still climb up and over. Nothing will induce them to stay outside.

~

It is said that ten days after the Bullfrog, *Pyxicephalus adspersus*, the largest of the toads, starts calling, rain will fall.

The Little Bush Squeaker, *Arthroleptis wahlbergi*, also starts calling when the first clouds of the season are piling up in the distance.

Reports of sudden appearances of frogs where none were before give rise to the saying, 'it rained frogs'. The explanation is simple. In autumn many species of frogs burrow deep into the ground or hide under rocks and hibernate for the winter, only emerging when it rains. Sometimes they are accidentally dislodged by labourers tilling or hoeing the fields in preparation for the planting of spring crops. Tradition insists that they be returned immediately to their burrows, otherwise unseasonable rain will fall. With the onset of heavy rain, after prolonged drought, the soil becomes soft and the frogs rapidly dig their way to the surface, and almost before the storm is over they suddenly appear, sometimes in incredible numbers. It is this extraordinary sight of seeing so many frogs where, shortly before, the land was dry and hard, that gives rise to fanciful notions, like the fantastic fable from Mozambique of where frogs go during the dry season.

It goes as follows:

One fine day, at the beginning of the dry season, the impala challenged the frog to a running competition. Naturally the impala won, and when he tried to claim his prize the frog said,

'Wait, give me a chance to win the next round! Can you rise from the dead? Burn my house from over my head and see what happens.'

So the following day the impala arrived at the frog's house and set fire to it. All the animals in the vicinity mourned the frogs, for they had been good neighbours.

After six months the rain came and soon the place where the frog houses had been was submerged. That evening when the impala came to drink he saw the frog in the water with his wife and surrounded by numerous frogs. The surprised impala demanded to know where the frog had been. The frog croaked,

'In the country of the dead, of course, since you killed us in the fire.'

'What is it like down there?' asked the impala.

'Oh, very pleasant! Don't you see we are all looking round and healthy? Look at our children, they were all born in the Land Under the Earth. The God of the Dead has blessed us!'

The impala, who had no children, was jealous, went home to his wife, and lit the walls of his house. He and his wife burned to ashes, for he did not know that frogs, in the dry season, dig themselves into the earth and sleep there until the rains come.

⁓

One of the best things about our place is the ever-flowing river in the valley, not just for the water it provides, but because it is free of bilharzia.

A fluke is not a hole in one, it's a flatworm which causes bilharzia, that dreaded dis-

The platanna, Xenopus laevis, is a slippery, tongueless, earless creature with no eyelids and monstrous thighs, but it is extremely useful to women who want to know if they're pregnant. About 2 cc of chemically treated urine from the expectant woman is injected into the female platanna, and within 6 to 12 hours, if it lays up to a few thousand eggs, then the answer is yes; if no eggs are laid, then the answer is no. Urine from pregnant women contains a hormone which stimulates frogs to lay eggs.

ease of African rivers. *Schistosoma haematobium* is a nasty little creature, 1–2 cm in length, which lives in the soft tissue near your bladder, while *S. japonicum* chooses the tiny blood vessels of your small intestine. As all things in nature must do, they go forth and multiply, so they mate and produce large quantities of spiky eggs, which rupture the delicate walls of the surrounding gut or bladder and escape the confines of the body via the faeces or urine.

The spiky eggs hatch in the water, releasing little ciliated larvae; these swim around looking for a special kind of snail which they have to find within a few hours if they are to survive. The snail, feeding contentedly off the rocks in the calm waters, is penetrated by these minute larvae, which feed on the soft tissue of the snail. The larvae undergo two more changes in their cycle, the first, a miracle of creation whereby it simply reorganises its molecules, providing a mass of yet another larval form. They, in turn, divide yet again, producing literally thousands of descendants from a single fluke.

These tiny creatures bore their way out of the now defunct snail and swim about in the water looking for a fisherman fishing, a woman doing her weekly wash or a child swimming. They will burrow into the skin of their mammalian host, enter the bloodstream and settle in the soft recesses of the human body to renew their cycle.

So whenever you see a group of children splashing in an African river, avoid the water like the plague, because if you don't, that's what you'll get.

~

The phrase 'halcyon days' comes from Greek mythology. Alcyone was the wife of Ceyx, who died in a shipwreck. In her grief she cast herself into the sea and the couple were changed into kingfishers. In the northern hemisphere the breeding of the kingfisher takes place during the calm fourteen days around the winter solstice. It was fabled to have a nest floating far out to sea, to charm the wind and the waves, to make the sea especially calm during that period. What happens in fact is that it goes not only out to sea, but across it, and finds a warmer continent on which to breed.

A Greek tragedy of unbridled violence is at the root of the dim-witted Helmeted Guineafowl acquiring its spots. Its scientific name is *Numida meleagris*. Numida was an ancient country in North Africa where guineafowl were plentiful. *Meleagris* is named after Meleager, the son of Oeneus, the King of Calydon, an ancient city in Aetolia (southern Italy). According to mythology Meleager led a party of hunters to kill the Aetolian boar, which had been sent by Artemis to ravage Calydon. Atlanta, also on the hunt, wounded the animal, so Meleager, being the leader, finished it off and sent the skin to Atlanta. Meleager's uncles disputed this, so Meleager killed them and then, in what must have been a mixture of grief and revenge, Meleager was killed by his own mother, who then, in remorse, hanged herself. The sisters of Meleager were so distraught that they turned into guineafowl, which to this day are covered with white tear drops.

Legend also tells us that the concretion of Meleager's sisters' tears is amber, the fossilised vegetable resin used in jewellery. It actually comes from extinct pine trees. The name 'amber' originally belonged to ambergris, which is a smelly wax-like secretion from the sperm whale. This rather takes the magic out of it, doesn't it?

Guineafowl

My cat brought me a Green Twinspot (*Mandingoa nitidula*).

I couldn't wait to count its spots.

Let me explain. There are two other species of twinspots in South Africa, the Red-throated and the Pink-throated, both with the name *Hypargos*. In Greek mythology, Argus was the hundred-eyed guardian of Io (*hypo* means below – having a hundred eyes below). Argus was sent by Hera, the wife of Zeus, to watch over Io, the daughter of Inachus, whom Zeus had turned into a

African Hoopoe

heifer to conceal from Hera his lust for Io. Argus was killed by Hermes on Zeus' instruction and Hera put the hundred eyes into the tail of her favourite bird, the peacock. Although Greek legends are confusing, how the taxonomists managed to confuse a peacock with a twinspot is not clear. I have dispatched my cat to catch the other two species because my twinspot has only 87 spots.

The name *Caprimulgus* (Latin, *caprus*, a goat; *mulgere*, to milk) is given to all nightjars, with the age-old misconception that nightjars suck the milk from goats. It probably stems from the observation that they have huge mouths and are always hanging around animal pens, attracted by the insects which are usually found near animals.

~

The suitably onomatopoeic name for the foul-smelling African Hoopoe is *Upupa africana*. Her nest is an unlined hole in the ground or hollow tree in which she sits for seventeen days. She has fairly relaxed sanitary arrangements and allows piles of droppings to accumulate in her unventilated nest. She also has an unpleasant odour emitting from the preen gland, which she spreads over her feathers during preening. If she or her chicks take fright they exude this smelly substance.

Never startle a hoopoe.

~

The Egyptians call the Sacred Ibis 'Father John'. It is the incarnation of the god Thoth, who in the guise of an ibis escaped the pursuit of Typhon. It is said to drink only the purest of water, and its feathers could scare or even kill the crocodile. It is also said that the bird is so fond of Egypt that it should pine to death if transported elsewhere. If, indeed, it devours crocodile eggs, scares away the crocodiles themselves, and devours serpents and all sorts of noxious reptiles and insects, no wonder it should be held in high regard, sacred in fact, and that killing it is considered a crime.

~

On meeting a solitary *Pachypodium namaquanum*, one should doff one's hat. Sometimes they appear in family groups as if frozen in their

Koekemakranka

Black-eyed Bulbul

march southwards. They are rare and grow in the sunbaked desert mountains of the northwestern Cape, where the fight for survival is at its harshest. To prevent precious moisture from being lost during its growing season, from August to October, it sports a ridiculous topknot of crinkled felt-like leaves, in the centre of which nestle tubular waxy wine-red flowers; these soon dry out and fall off during the hot summer months. To ensure maximum utilisation of the sun's rays, the crowns of the plants, without exception, bend towards the north at an angle of 30°.

The Nama people have a romantic, rather forlorn explanation. 'Years ago their ancestors lived north of the Great Orange [now the Gariep] River and had to flee southwards from their enemies. When they had crossed the mighty river, those who had turned round and looked back at the land they had to leave, were turned to stone, with their anguished faces ever turned towards the north. There they stand sentinel-like rooted to the spot and are known as the "half-mens."'

But the nicest name of all, to my ears, is the Koekemakranka. The name is used for all the members of the *Gethyllis* genus, more specifically for *Gethyllis spiralis*, whose curly leaves are designed to prevent moisture loss, with fifty per cent of the surface always being turned away from the sun. The swollen seed-pod adds a tasty kick to local home-brewed brandy.

The early warning system of the Black-eyed Bulbul is effective in announcing the presence of a snake or a cat. He perches above the offending danger and shouts, 'take-no-notice! take-no-notice!', which impresses upon my memory, indelibly, contrarily, its scientific name, *Pycnonotus barbatus*. There he goes again, 'Pycnonotus, take-no-notice, Pycnonotus, take-no-notice!'

When I see a bush completely wrapped up with spider's web I remember a story, which originates in Ghana, about Anansi the Spider.

One day a veld fire raged. All the animals desperately sought an escape from the flames. A fleeing buck heard a tiny voice, 'Please let me sit in your ear so that we can escape together!'

It was Anansi the Spider who, without waiting for an answer, jumped down from a branch and settled in the antelope's ear. The flames came closer and she panicked, for she could not see a way out, but the spider whispered, 'Go left, now go straight on ... ', until the buck's swift legs had carried them both to safety.

When the fire was far behind them, the spider ran down the antelope's leg, saying, 'Thank you very much for your kindness, we shall meet again sometime.'

Not long afterwards, the antelope gave birth to a baby antelope, which, as all students of nature know, spends its first few days hiding under a bush while the mother grazes some distance away.

Suddenly two hunters with bows and arrows spotted the mother and gave chase. She was faster than they were, so she outwitted them. The hunters returned to the place where they had first seen the buck, hoping to find her calf. They searched in vain and left. After a few hours, the worried and weary mother returned but could not find her child. Then she heard a familiar voice calling her. It was Anansi the Spider, who led her to a bush which was covered by a dense network of spider's web. Inside, quite safe and fast asleep, was the little antelope.

Now, every time I see the huge web of a Communal Spider I wonder if there's a springbok calf inside.

Late in the eighteenth century Princess Helena of Spain sent an explorer to Africa where, in the bushveld grasslands of Zululand, he walked into a web woven by the Golden Orb Web Spider (*Nephila*). The spider itself is an attractive specimen, having a large colourful abdomen, but the web to the explorer was so beautiful that he gathered handfuls of the stuff to take home to his princess. She was duly impressed and ordered him to return to Africa and collect enough web so that she could have a pair of golden boots made from the silk.

Another of the Princess's explorers was sent to Cuba where he collected for her one of the smallest birds in the world, Princess Helena's Coquette (*Mellisuga helenae*), a stuffed specimen of which is on display at the South African Museum in Cape Town.

The Grey Penduline Tit, *Anthoscopus caroli*, the 'carolus' part being the Latinised form of the name Charles, was named after Charles John Andersson, Swedish of birth and giant of character. Having read his account of his encounters with dangerous wild beasts, deprivation and hardship in the heart of darkest Africa, I feel he deserves a bird with more dignity to its name.

Descriptive names have been given to an unjustly
maligned family. Who can fail to be enthralled by a group
of creatures with names such as:

VIOLIN

GARBAGE

WEDDING CAKE

LEAF CURLING

CANNIBAL

WHITE LADY

PIRATE

WIDOW

QUICKSILVER

BOX KITE

MONEY

PYJAMA

FEATHER-LEGGED

ZEBRA

JUMPING

FISHERMAN

DANDY

FIDDLE-BACKED

FOUR-LUNG

BIRD-DROPPING

TWO-LUNG

COMB-FOOTED

LUNGLESS

OGRE-FACED

TROPICAL TENT

PALP-FOOTED

TWO-EYED,

SIX-EYED,

EIGHT-EYED,

FOUR-JAWED

BUTTON AND BABOON

AND, OF COURSE,

DADDY-LONGLEGS.

Nephila

Fish-eating spider

Mind you, the Grey Penduline Tit does build an admirable nest. It is a compact composition of woolly substances from plants and animals, tightly woven into a felt-like material, with a little awning which closes easily over the protruding entrance, and below it an open false pocket, used as a perch by the incoming bird. As it opens the entrance with one foot, the entrance tube closes automatically, forming a roof over the ledge, and resulting in a 'false entrance', supposed to mislead snakes into thinking that the nest is empty.

Understandably, butterflies have been given colourful names. Consider the Striped Policeman, the Lemon Traveller, the Topaz Arab, the Poplar Leopard, the Streaked Sailor, Pirate, Woolly-legs, the Dismal Sylph, the Apricot Playboy, the Joker, the Polka Dot, the Friar, Black-pie, Black Heart, Bush Nightfighter, Foxtrot Copper, the Wandering and Confusing Sandman, the Seaside Skolly and Mrs Raven's Flat. Now who on earth was Mrs Raven?

~

Just as much fun are some names for groups of moths – like the Handmaidens and Prominents, Brahmins and Emperors, Eggars and Monkeys, Loopers and Hooktips, Slugs, Goats, Owls and Tigers.

Their common names are imaginative and exotic. Visualise a Luminous Cloud, a Frowning Tigerlet and an Edible Monkeys; however, they all describe pale drab little creatures hardly worth a second glance. Names like the Squinting Tabby and Similar Shark, Dappled Custard and Sliced Chocolate, Lunar Eclipse, and the Spacious and Dejected Goat and, of course, the Horrid Flame, all suggest insects with character but they too are nothing to write home about.

The Emperors, which are amongst the largest and handsomest of all the moths, hardly earn their stripes with names like Cavorting, Confused and Injured Emperors.

One of the most widely distributed of all butterflies in southern Africa is the African Monarch, *Danaus chrysippus*. When it's a caterpillar its food plant is the milkweed, which contains cardenolides (heart poisons), not toxic to caterpillars but most distasteful to birds and lizards. When the caterpillar turns into a butterfly it retains this toxicity in its body, and the predator, after tasting it only once, avoids it or anything like it. (If you need to tell the difference between a male and female, the male Monarch has four black spots on its hind wing and the female has only three.)

Another butterfly species, which in its caterpillar stage does not choose to eat from the milkweed and would therefore be highly palatable to predators, has, through evolution, come to resemble, almost identically, *Danaus chrysippus*. This remarkable butterfly is the female *Hypolimnas misippus*, or aptly named 'mimic'. But since butterfly predators can't count, the mimic has only one spot on its hind wing.

If you are a lepidopterist you will notice that only the placement of four black dots will help you to tell your *chrysippus* from your *misippus*.

However, if you are a male *Hypolimnas misippus*, and if you have avoided being eaten by predators, and since evolution chose to colour you black with white spots, you will have to rely on body language to help you recognise a possible mate. The male *Hypolimnas*, unable to count spots, sits and waits for anything large and orange to fly past. Once he spots something that looks promising he flies along hopefully a few centimetres beneath it. If he is lucky and it is indeed a female *Hypolimnas*, she will recognise this subtle approach and the unmistakeable black and white wings, and will settle on the ground inviting the male to mate with her. But if it is a female *Danaus chrysippus* that the *Hypolimnas misippus* has mistakenly chosen to court, she will just ignore him. She only responds to a more direct approach by the male *Danaus*, who is not only the same colour as she is, but boldly announces his attentions by beating her about the abdomen with his antennae, which emit a distinctive pheromone positively identifying him.

There is yet another orange contender to confuse the issue, riding on the back of *Danaus*, so to speak: the female *Papilio dardanus cenea* looks very similar to the female *Danaus*, even to the extent of sacrificing the wearing of the elegant swallowtails which are usually diagnostic of its species. Its flight too is slow, like that of *Danaus*, preferring the shade of the forest.

To further confuse the male swallowtail, and us, some female *Papilio dardanus*

Male *Danaus chrysippus*

Female *Danaus chrysippus*

Female *Hypolimnas misippus* (mimic)

Male *Hypolimnas misippus*

ceneas choose to sport black and white wings.

The male *Papilio dardanus* cenea remains a typical pale yellow and black swallowtail.

The smallish look-alike to *Danaus chrysippus* from Zimbabwe, Mozambique and further north is the *Mimacrea marshalli* and it too has the leisurely gliding flight of *Danaus,* and also untypical of its *Acraea* family in that it feeds off lichens.

A footnote in this maze of deception is the White barred *Acraea encedon,* trying its best to imitate *Danaus chrysippus,* which is hardly necessary, because being an *Acraea,* it exudes a foul-tasting yellow fluid anyway, hydrogen cyanide, which adequately protects it from predators.

While I am cognisant of the fact that nature is a world of deception and camouflage, my favourite animal, the cheetah, has a coat of spots so delicious to paint that I risk repetition in my coverage of this superb creature.

chapter six

FUNCHAL CAFE

FOR
FRIED FISH & CHIPS
TAKE·AWAYS
REFRESHMENTS
FANCY GOODS
GROCERRIES
MEDECINES

on

Eating

Dis-moi ce que tu manges, je te dirai ce que tu est.
(Tell me what you eat and I will tell you who you are.)
— BRILLAT-SAVARIN,
EIGHTEENTH-CENTURY POLITICIAN AND GOURMET

The Kudu is a fussy feeder, requiring a wide variety of plants from which he can nibble, seldom stopping for more than a minute or two before moving on to the next bush. There is a reason for this.

Some plants have fairly high tannin levels in their leaves and these are avoided by the Kudu. Tannin is used commercially for curing leather to make handbags, belts and shoes. The Kudu, in his prime, is not ready to be made into shoes and handbags, so he naturally chooses plants with little or no tannin. However, the cunning plant has an extraordinary technique of raising its tannin level within minutes of being browsed. In *Acacia caffra*, for instance, the tannin level in the leaves doubles within fifteen minutes. If the Kudu moves on, the level drops back to normal within two or three days. But if the Kudu herd is trapped in a restricted area and has repeatedly to return to the same tree before the level of tannin has dropped, the protein-based enzymes which are responsible for digesting the leaves form an inert tannin-protein complex. So the Kudu, having eaten tannin-laden leaves, may have a full belly but derives no nutrients from the meal and can eventually starve to death. No wonder the Kudu moves quickly to the next unsuspecting bush. But wait, the next bush is not as unsuspecting as one would expect. The browsed bush is able to transmit a 'warning' of the advancing browser to its neighbours by releasing aromatic compounds into the air and the tannin levels in the nearby plants are raised.

So, if you see a Kudu galloping from tree to tree grabbing a leaf here, a leaf there, he's only trying to outwit the rising tide of tannin.

~

The beautiful butterfly is the symbol of the soul but has deplorable habits and disgusting table manners. Watch closely a congregation of butterflies sipping water from the edge of a spring or seepage point. You will see that the whole time they are drinking there is a continual squirting of drops of water from their rear. They are pumping the water through their bodies,

Cane rat

extracting from it minute quantities of mineral salts. Although some species do sip nectar genteelly from flowers, others have a taste for engine oil, rotten bananas, alcohol, blood and excrement, particularly, so I am told, lion dung.

The anomalies of our microcosmic piece of Africa prove only that statistics are not to be trusted. The endangered and habitat-specific Red Duiker is to be seen almost every day making its way to the river across the tarred road, whereas the Greater Cane Rat (*Thryonomys swinderianus*) is one of the most common small mammals and, in our neck of the woods, is seldom seen. One was caught in a trap put out for house rats and we were astonished when we saw our first cane rat. It was aggressive and clearly very frightened, so we let it go, which was lucky for him, because we heard later that the Zulus love to eat them. Conveniently, if handled, their hair falls out, ready for the pot, so to speak. Adult male cane rats not only eat their own young if locked up together, but promiscuous ones rip to shreds any reluctant females.

According to Professor Anne Alexander they would make an excellent source of protein to help alleviate malnutrition and starvation in Africa if farmed under controlled conditions. At present, however, they are a delicacy, highly prized in gourmet restaurants and are, I believe, absolutely delicious.

In Natal, where sugarcane cutters were unhappy about the snakes that lived in the cane fields, they chased out and killed the last remaining snake, including the harmless ones. The result was a huge proliferation of cane rats, which, having no predators, chewed their way through the sugar crop. The farmers had to reintroduce the snakes.

Invariably causing a shudder of revulsion in most people, the cockroach should be given credit for having survived the carboniferous period, 300 million years ago. Although they themselves are clean, they tend to scavenge in refuse and sewage, thereby contaminating food and transmitting diseases.

There is a certain cockroach which lives in my paint drawer and is attracted to substances, perhaps the glycerine, in certain colours. I use a mixture of Cobalt blue and Vandyke brown for painting the eyes of birds and animals. If the finished paintings are

pinned to the board on the wall overnight, unprotected by plastic covers, the next morning I will find the eyes have been completely eaten away.

Some cockroaches do not have the necessary enzymes to break down plant cellulose, so they have established symbiotic relationships with micro-organisms which live in their intestines and do their digesting for them.

Well, really!

~

The story of the male sandgrouse saturating its breast-feathers in water, and then flying back to its chicks waiting patiently in their nests fifty kilometres away, is absurd. Why don't they lay their eggs closer to the water? However, since it is so, scientists have not to question why, but how. An experiment with sandgrouse chicks in the laboratory showed that they will not take drinking water from an eyedropper but will only suck from wet cotton wool. The belly feathers of the Namaqua Sandgrouse (*Pterocles namaqua*), because of their highly specified bar-bules, not only hold three times as much water as the corresponding feathers of other birds, but maintained their structure in spite of regular wetting and sucking. A normal feather would soon begin to fray as a result. I think it's so that the female can get some peace from the constant call for 'kelkiewyn-kelkiewyn-kelkiewyn'.

~

Caring for a creature of nocturnal habits has it disadvantages. On hearing that we were interested in creatures great and small, a neighbour brought us a brindly beast. It was a displaced orphaned Water Mongoose, about four months old. When I tried to pick it up, it barked and bit me. We offered it some minced raw chicken and milk; both were greedily accepted. Our neighbour believed he had done us a favour. Two weeks of chaos. I was under the illusion that all orphans would be cuddly, cute and grateful. During the day it burrowed into my cupboards tearing up papers and soiling my clothes. At night it ran around yelping and scratching and trying to catch beetles. It had an insatiable appetite and a nervous disposition, so its dilemma of whether to

The Aardwolf is the only animal for which there is no English name.

The Ant-eating Chat, Myrmecocichla formicivora, *forms a feeding association with the Aardwolf, which is hardly fair because the Aardwolf has to eat 300 000 termites a night to keep the wolf from the door.*

accept the food I offered or to shriek at me made it most unlovable. Because of its bristly coat it wasn't nice to touch and yet it wanted affection. It crept hesitantly towards us and make gentle throaty noises if we stroked it. But if we made a quick movement it would bark loudly and dive behind something. Although we knew that Water Mongooses lived near water, we were worried that there might not be enough food in our small stream. The fish in our little dam were very small but there were plenty of crabs; so we put him in a closed basket early one evening and took him down to the river. He took to the riverine bushes immediately. We watched until it was quite dark. Our last view of him was with a crab in his front paws, so we made our way home by torchlight.

One abhors wars for obvious reasons, but the Anglo-Boer War of 1899–1902 shall also be remembered for marking the introduction to South Africa, in forage imported from South America, of the foul-smelling, ubiquitous, small, light-brown Argentine Ant (*Iridomyrmex humilis*). It has become a serious pest in urban areas and has displaced indigenous species in others.

Fortunately there are many types of myrmecophagus (ant- and termite-eating) creatures. A great number of ants have to be consumed to satisfy even the smallest appetite, so it is advisable to form a partnership in the quest for lunch. The Antbear or Aardvark (*Orycteropus afer*) and two Clapper Larks (*Mirafra apiata*) have also been observed hunting together.

The Aardwolf is an unfortunate, inconsequential creature, not one of the Big Five, relentlessly hunted because of the completely erroneous belief that it is destructive to stock and dangerous to Man.

Mealtime symbiosis also happens with ants and butterflies.

The larvae of some *Aloeides* sp. butterflies release a pheromone which mimics the pheromones ants use for communication, misleading the ants into believing the butterfly larvae to be their own brood. Sometimes the larvae remain inside the antheap and eat the ants' eggs, but sometimes they emerge at night to feed on their own food plant, accompanied by a battalion of ant 'bodyguards'. A butterfly reserve near Roodepoort has been established to protect *Aloeides dentatis*, this rare and extraordinary butterfly.

The Greater Honeyguide (*Indicator indicator*) is a parasitic bird, deviously expropriating someone else's nest or exploiting a *ratel*. The first misdemeanour is accomplished by well-coordinated teamwork. The male honeyguide, pretending to be a hawk, bombs the nest of a barbet or hoopoe. As a result the bird flees in self-preservation, being deluded for just long enough for the female honeyguide to lay her egg. The egg develops so rapidly that it stands a good chance of hatching before the hosts' eggs.

The Greater Honeyguide

Aardvark

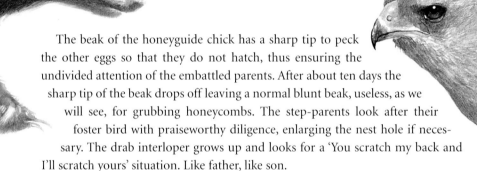

Honey Badger

The beak of the honeyguide chick has a sharp tip to peck the other eggs so that they do not hatch, thus ensuring the undivided attention of the embattled parents. After about ten days the sharp tip of the beak drops off leaving a normal blunt beak, useless, as we will see, for grubbing honeycombs. The step-parents look after their foster bird with praiseworthy diligence, enlarging the nest hole if necessary. The drab interloper grows up and looks for a 'You scratch my back and I'll scratch yours' situation. Like father, like son.

When a honeyguide finds a bees' nest it seeks out an accomplice hive-thief by spreading its tail, thereby exposing a white tail pattern, followed by a flight display of downward and upward swoops, usually in a circle, making at the same time a 'tschukka-tschukka' noise. (The sound may be imitated by us, if we are so inclined, by rattling a half-empty matchbox lengthwise.) The honeyguide is not interested in the honey, but in the wax, the bees, the grubs and their larvae.

In the unlikely event of your being invited by the honeyguide to participate in his quest for the bees' nest, it would be well to remember to emit little grunts as you follow. This is customary, nay obligatory, if you are to maintain the right relationship with the bird. This is, of course, because it's the sound that a Honey Badger makes as it trots purposefully behind the honeyguide.

The Honey Badger (*Mellivora capensis*) is a shy, retiring, but co-operative creature, with a varied diet of roots, bulbs and fruit, small animals, snakes, frogs and scorpions, and with an insatiable weakness for honey. It has sharp claws and a hide impervious to stings. In spite of its heavy bulk it is able to climb trees to reach the bees' nest, which it breaks open with its claws. Once the hive is open the honeyguide moves in and claims the loot.

*Pale Chanting
Goshawk*

Hovering nearby, in the Gang of Four, is the Pale Chanting Goshawk, always watchful for any grubs or larvae that the Honey Badger may have disturbed or left behind.

At the scene of the crime there may also be a pile of dead honeybees. Some honey hunters claim the *ratel* uses its anal gland to fumigate the beehives, the way people use smoke. Reversing towards the hive's entrance hole, the *ratel* spreads a smelly secretion with its swirling tail, suffocating and stupefying the bees.

The fourth accomplice is the jackal, the nervous tail-ender, ready to scavenge and run.

There is no honour amongst thieves, they say. Legend has it that if the Honey Badger eats all the booty before the honey guide has had its share, the next time there is a honeycomb raid, the honeyguide will lead the Honey Badger and his cronies straight into the jaws of a lion.

The Capped Wheatear's curious habit of bowing exaggeratedly on landing and flicking his tail up and down, bobbing and making clicking calls, could suggest that the poor fellow is simply still trying to get out of the bird-lime.

The name Wheatear has nothing to do with wheat or ears but was originally 'white arse'.

Jackal

How the Honeyguide came to have authority over honey

Honeyguide and Capped Wheatear lived together in one place and ate out of one dish. Honeyguide was the elder, Wheatear the younger. They set their minds on going to hunt for honey, and when they arrived at the place where they knew there was a bees' nest, Honeyguide said, 'Smile, Wheatear, when you can see where the honey is.'

After a while Wheatear smiled, but he had not seen the honey. Honeyguide spotted the honey and smiled. They returned home leaving the honey behind, but Wheatear secretly disappeared and went off to steal the honey.

Next morning Honeyguide said, 'Let's go to our honey.'

There they found a bit of bare honeycomb mangled and thrown about, so Honeyguide asked Wheatear about it, and Wheatear replied, 'My brother, I do not know who could have done this thing.'

So Honeyguide said no more, and they went out again looking for honey. Once more they found some honey. This time Honeyguide saw it first and he tested Wheatear by saying,

'Why do you not smile, have you not seen the honey?'

Wheatear replied that he had not yet seen the honey, although by now he had. He said to Honeyguide, 'You did not believe me yesterday and you do not believe me again today. Let us bring some bird-lime and set a trap for the honey thief.'

Honeyguide agreed and went off to get some bird-lime from the humans. When they arrived at the village, Honeyguide said, 'We will go tomorrow to set the trap.'

After a while Honeyguide disappeared and went off to set the bird-lime at the place of the honey. Wheatear said to himself, 'Let me go quietly and eat the honey.' But the bird-lime was already set, although he did not notice it. When he thought of sitting down beside the honey, he sat on the bird-lime.

Said he, 'I will strike it with my wing.' But he stuck to it with his wing and nearly lost his balance. And when he struck with his tail he stuck to it with his tail. He tried to strike it with his breast but he stuck fast.

To this day it is the Honeyguide whose honey-detecting skills are extolled and the Wheatear who has to forage on the ground for insects.

One of the most irritating insects is the mosquito.

It is only the female mosquito which relies on the blood of mammals to produce her eggs successfully. She has heat-sensitive antennae capable of sensing differences in temperature of only one five-hundredth of a degree Celsius, several metres away. She swivels her antennae until the amount of heat stimulus on each one is equal, thereby getting a fix on her prospective victim. As she gets closer to her target she picks up its scent to guide her on the last stage of her journey.

The male, you'll be happy to know, only sucks plant juices.

Humans vary in the amount of heat they give off. Those giving off a lot of warmth attract mosquitoes to themselves best, and the person who gets excited and throws his arms around, driving up his own temperature, is only playing into the hands of the female mosquito. Clothing, especially black, allows heat to escape more readily into the surrounding air: white clothing therefore helps to keep female mosquitoes at bay.

There are anti-mosquito ointments, lotions and sprays, but all lose their efficacy as soon as you sweat, changing the smell – I beg your pardon, the scent – you give off. A simple remedy is to carry around an aerosol tin of hard-hold hair lacquer and spray the delicate little chap into a solid immobile object, thereby fouling his props, and he will drop like a rock.

~

African rivers have a magic of their own. Kipling found it in his 'great grey green greasy Limpopo all set about with fever trees'.

Water is precious in Africa, so it is inevitable that, in almost every pool or stream, a spirit dwells, usually a benevolent one. In bigger rivers and lakes there are also spirits, darker and more foreboding, the symbolism arising from the prevalence of drownings in deeper waters. However, for me, rivers hold no sinister implications, just the promise of life-giving irrigation for thirsty lands, and cool, shady, tree-lined banks.

So one of our first major purchases was a pair of canoes. None of us had ever canoed before, but unhesitatingly we launched ourselves from the causeway into the

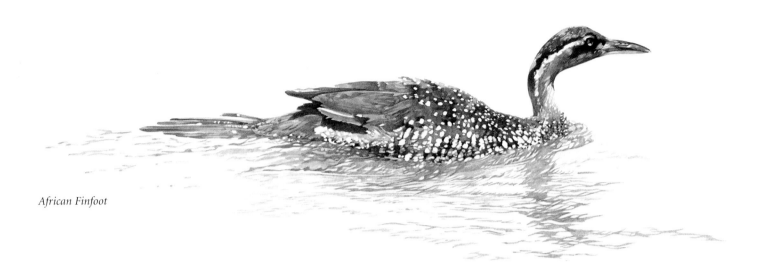

African Finfoot

unknown waters of the Crocodile River. We took to the gentle flow like fallen leaves. Giant Kingfishers barely blinked as we passed, herons merely paused in their probing, an African Finfoot glided shyly out of sight.

The flow of the river coaxed us on, faster and faster.

Manoeuvring the canoes between boulders requires quick thinking, good balance and agility, but when a large great grey boulder takes a dive and disappears under the water, one needs nerves of steel.

I hadn't thought to ask anyone if there were any hippos in the river.

It is often said by people who should know, that hippos are responsible for more human deaths than any other wild animal in Africa. The dominant male hippo marks his territory by scattering his dung in the water, on bushes and rocks, by flicking his tail with a vigorous sideways movement. 'It hits the fan.'

According to an African legend, the Great Spirit granted the Hippopotamus permission to live both on the land and in the water, but because hippos have such huge mouths, He was concerned that they might eat all the fish. He therefore made them promise to eat only vegetation, and in order to make sure that they complied with His decree, He made them scatter their dung so that He could check it periodically to see whether it contained any fish bones.

~

The odours characteristic of various foods may not be of the foods themselves but the result of the atmospheric oxidation of substances present in them. The aroma of roasting coffee beans is more appealing than the taste of the coffee itself, and the smell of bacon frying in the pan exceeds the taste, which, let's face it, is not bad at the best of times.

In the late afternoon in the Lowveld and Natal there is often a distinctive and evocative smell of potatoes cooking. It comes from a nondescript climber-shrub called *Philanthus reticulatus*, and no matter what part of the plant you crush, be it the berry, the leaf or the flower, not a whiff is produced. But walk a few metres away and there it is. Purely the oxidation with the atmosphere.

Almonds, the most delectable of nuts, have, ironically, the smell associated with suspect mushrooms, arsenic and the *bitteramandelboom* (*Brabejum stellatifolium*), which is the tree proclaimed, not only as the tree to have caused the first fatal case recorded in South Africa of human poisoning, but also as a National Monument. In 1660 Jan van Riebeeck planted a hedge of wild *bitteramandelboomen* around the settlement below Table Mountain to protect the small group of farmers against raiding, 'so thick that neither cattle nor sheep could be driven through it'. Fragments of this hedge still grow in the Kirstenbosch National Botanical Garden in Cape Town.

Little Sparrowhawk bathing

We South Africans think of bobotie (curried mince with almonds on top) as the very essence of old Cape cuisine. Dr C. Louis Leipoldt came across a recipe for bobotie under that same name in an old Italian cookery book. In fact it was a favourite dish of Richard Coeur de Lion back in the twelfth century, and according to *Traditional Fare of England and Wales* it was still a popular dish in the middle of the eighteenth century.

Isn't it strange that wives who live in the country are expected to have larders stocked with homemade jams, pickles and bottled fruit? So to show off to my city supermarket friends I decided to make gingerbeer. I found Grandma's recipe and set to work smugly stirring the sugary syrup, recalling Grandma's stories of how the corks popped off in the night. 'Well, these are the nineties, Doda,' said I to myself as I tight-

ened the last of the screw tops onto the glass bottles. No popping of corks now. Modern technology has provided us with a perfect sealer to make for extra-fizzy gingerbeer. Through the weeks I watched the swollen raisins dancing playfully between the beaded bubbles at the surface of the promising nectar. And it came to pass that on the morning of the third week I was in my studio painting the delicate neck feathers of a Cut-throat Finch when there was an almighty explosion.

Yes, you're right, the seals held, but the bottles didn't.

That is not the end of the story.

The problem now was what to do with a dozen or so lethal gingerbeer grenades whose pins had been pulled. You consult the experts, that's what. Harry (the expert) was quick to grasp the gravity of the situation. Looking like an astronaut, with a camping mattress roped to his body, a motorbike helmet on his head, leather gloves clutching a snake-catching looped stick, he presented a formidable opponent to the enemy. Needless to say, all bottles were diffused safely and we drank flat gingerbeer for weeks. I am still scouring the sticky syrup off the rough-plastered pantry walls and scouring the antique shops for stoneware jars like Granny used to have.

Some people have claimed that drinking lemon juice is a cause of cancer. Others recommend lemon as a seasickness cure but, they add, if it is not effective, at least it tastes no worse coming up than it did going down.

You should never cut parsley when you are in love. If you give it away you give away your luck; nor should you accept it as a gift: if you must have it, buy or steal it.

⌣

As the name suggests, *Pachypodium succulentum*, or *dikvoet*, as it is known, is delicious. It is an underground tuber about 25 cm in diameter, from which short succulent stems sprout and these are eaten by hunter-gatherers in the drier parts of South Africa. Superstition again prevails and demands that, prior to being eaten, it must first be thrown over the right shoulder to destroy the 'bitter or poisonous principle'.

Pachys means thick or stout in Greek, so I am reminded, in passing, of a pachyderm, which is of course an elephant, though the thick skin does not, it seems, apply to their psyche. Opie and Tatum, in their dictionary of superstitions, say that any drawings or carvings of elephants must always be placed in a room so their heads face

the door, as they become wild if they do not know what is
going on.

Poets establish metaphors which become norms, but
not all plants follow the dictates of the poets.

'The fragrance of a flower' when applied to a stapeliad
is directed only to flies. To us, it stinks.

The Stapeliadeacae is a bizarre group of plants which have
flowers the colour and odour of rotten meat. They also have little
hairs which entangle the struggling fly in its attempt to leave once he
discovers he has been duped. The more he struggles, the more the
pollen sticks to his legs. Contrary to popular belief neither the
stapeliad nor the Venus Fly Trap eats the fly.

The fly is also attracted to smelly fungi such as *Aseroe rubra*, *Amanita
muscaria*, *Phallus rubicundus* and *Clathrus archeri*. The spores are the
smelly, brown, faeces-like sticky stuff in the centre of the fungus.

That insect dispersal of spores or pollen is the reason for the bad
smells in fungi and stapeliads is understandable, but growing along the banks
of our stream is a tree all but knocking you out with its stench. It is curiously named
Clausena anisata, suggesting aniseed, an agreeable ingredient in curries, but is more
appropriately called *perdepis* (horse pee). Its smell has also been likened to the 'smell
of the striped field-mouse', which 'stinks so strong that the hyena would not come near
it'. In spite of its smell, the tree is much valued as a magical and medicinal tree. Newborn babies are strengthened by being suspended in the smoke from burning branches; and to cleanse the body internally, strengthen the heart, cure rheumatism and
fevers, and to kill tapeworms, one should absorb the steam rising from the boiling
leaves of the malodorous plant.

Zorilla ictonyx striatus, more commonly seen as a squashed pile of black and white
fur on the tarred roads in the Karoo, than as the pretty little animal it is, has the nasty
habit of emitting a stream of unutterably foul-smelling liquid from its anal glands. It
is said that if a Zorilla approaches a lion kill, the lions back away and wait for the Zorilla to eat his fill and leave before they will return to their carcass.

On a distant mountaintop Liz, a notable naturalist, has a family of Rock Dassies (*Procavia capensis*) living in her house, and without being trained to do so, they use the family toilet. In the wild, dassies have special areas in the rocks which are demarcated latrine areas. The white streaks on cliff faces usually indicate the presence of a wild dassie colony. This white stuff, caused by leaching from the urine and faeces, is regarded by many African tribes as a treatment for kidney and liver problems and is even said to cure 'hysterical attacks'.

~

I am a cat lover, but when I see the look in the eyes of my cat as he squats in the sand, I grudgingly recognise a grain of truth in an entry in a twelfth-century Latin bestiary, which says that a lynx buries its urine out of a constitutional meanness. The lynx knows that its urine hardens into a precious stone called ligure and the medieval monks believed that the cat's disdain of the human race forces it to cover up its urine

in the sand as much as it can, lest it serve as an ornament to any human being.

The last word on this indelicate subject is a tale of the temerity of the diminutive Damara Dik-dik, which lives in the chalky white dust of the northwestern desert areas. Standing a mere 40 cm at the shoulder and with the innocence of a Disney doe, the wide-eyed, dark-lashed dik-dik is responsible for those huge, road-blocking dung-heaps. Science will say it's natural, 'security in numbers' behaviour, but I prefer the interpretation of the 'collective vendetta'.

Once upon a time, long, long ago 'a dik-dik stumbled over an elephant's dung-ball lying in its path and was so angry that from that time on, all dik-dik have deposited their rice-sized droppings in mounds, in the hope that an elephant would trip and thus avenge the indignity suffered by the stumbling dik-dik.'

on Other things

The wafer-waisted waif
with the withered wrists
writhed and wriggled
through the window,
and on a whim,
wafted away on the wind.

MAN CANNOT LIVE ON FOOD ALONE. As human beings we need to believe in something; to search for meanings, to question, to gamble, to interpret. Beyond the practicalities of life is a world of mystique and intrigue.

Inexplicable phenomena have always been given supernatural significance or religious connotations, but it is through the Science of Nature that all shall be revealed.

In the bleak wastes of Yakurdia in Siberia, there occurs a miracle of retribution. Beneath the snow and frozen rock, an abundance of diamonds was discovered. Inhabitants say that when God flew over Yakurdia, He felt so sorry for the freezing Yakurds that He wept and diamonds were born from His tears.

Similarly in those arid areas of Namaqualand where, for eleven months of the year, only gravel and sand crunch underfoot, the scene changes to a psychedelic explosion of colour when the spring rains fall. The legend in these parts is that God in His anger created the desert, and when He saw what He had done He relented and sprinkled it with flowers.

There are many plants whose flowers, like shops in France, open for relatively short intervals at specific times of the day – open for business, so to speak. What self-respecting mesembryanthemum would dream of opening before 10 a.m.?

The Perdevygie (*Trichodiadema pomeridianum*) opens from 2 to 4 p.m.; Tierbek-vygie (*Stomatium ermininum*) opens from 4 to 6 p.m.; the S'keng-keng (*Rabiea albino-ta*) opens from 2 to 5 p.m.; the Stryvygie (*Nananthus vittatus*) opens from 2 to 5 p.m.; and the Klein-s'keng-keng (*Bergeranthus glenesis*) only opens her petals from 2 to 5 p.m. Both the Vetkousie (*Carpanthea pomeridiana*) and the Snotwortel (*Cinicosia pugioniformis*) open from 1 p.m. to sunset and *Lithops lesliei* from 3 to 6 p.m.

Some open towards evening or at night to attract night-flying moths. *Conophytum truncatum* and *C. translucens* open at 8 p.m.; *C. odoratum* opens from 10 p.m. until the early hours of the morning. Others are so precise that you could set your clock by them, that is, if the sun is shining, because like the sundial there are limitations. Flowers require a certain amount of irradiation by the sun's rays, and unless that particular amount is forthcoming they simply do not open.

*The legend in Namaqualand is
that God in His anger created
the desert, and when He saw
what He had done He relented
and sprinkled it with flowers.*

The more vivid the scarlet, or coppery the red, or steely the blue, to the colouring of the lower face of the petals of the species with yellow or white flowers, the more they seem to be affected by the vagaries of solar radiation. How many busloads of eager tourists have driven across the country to see one of the seven wonders of the floral kingdom, Namaqualand, only to find that the promised spectacle is closed for the day?

The common white arum lily (*Zantedeschia aethiopica*) grows in the bog down by the stream. The rhizomes are eaten by the Bushpigs, the leaves soothe insect bites, and the Xhosa people drape a warmed leaf over their foreheads to cure a severe headache. On a cold day I can be found warming my hands around their soft white spathes.

In 1800 a certain Mr Hubert stated that a thermometer placed in the centre of five spadices of *Arum cordifolium* stood at 55°C, and in twelve at 61°C, while the temperature of the air was only 23.6°C. This showed an elevation of 13° and 20°. Through the years many experiments were conducted by different people in varying ways and all ascertained that there is a decided elevation of temperature within the flowers of the arum family, the highest being from 10°C to 20°C for the larger species, and proportionately less for the smaller ones.

At that most hallowed of botanic gardens, Kew, Mr Nicholson noted, of the Ivory Palm (*Phytelephas macrocarpa*), 'On April 20th 1881, at one p.m., the temperature of the house was 20°C, the bulb of a thermometer, which had been suspended for some time near the plant in question, was placed in the centre of the cream-coloured inflorescence, and the mercury almost instantly rose to 33.3°C, showing an increase in temperature of 4.4°C. The following day, at the same hour, the thermometer registered 22°C in the house, and, when placed in the same position in the centre of the inflorescence, only rose to the same height as that reached the preceding day, viz. 33.3°C. As the drawn-out end of the bulb prevented it from actually touching the convex ovaries, a small incision was made in one of these, and the thermometer then rose to 34.4°C.'

I don't know who or how they measured this but I heard that cattle give off 49 kilos of methane per year and sheep 7.2. Man's technology is blamed for the thinning ozone layer and global warming, but perhaps for the real cause we should look to the gaseous cows and feverish flowers.

By the way, a cousin to the arum lily, in the same family Araceae, is the *Colocasia*

antiquorum (var. *esculenta*), a tuber introduced into South Africa from the Pacific and now cultivated in most parts of the country. Commonly known as the *amadumbe* by the Zulus, it has a nutty flavour that is enjoyed in soups, biscuits, breads and puddings. However, in Watt and Breyer-Brandwijk's *Medicinal and Poisonous Plants of Southern and Eastern Africa* (1962), an authoritative tome on medicinal plants, we are cautioned that 'the consumption of *Colocasia* is believed to have a definite relationship to the causation of leprosy'.

Hesperanthas

The Arum Frog (*Hyperolius horstockii*), the Yellowstriped Reed Frog (*H. semidiscus*) and the Spiny Reed Frog (*Afrixalus fornasinii*) often sit inside an arum lily flower with their feet on the spathe and their backs against the flower column, or spadix, so that the frog's back becomes liberally covered with pollen. These warmth-seeking creatures also revel in sunbathing and can be found sleeping in exposed situations on a blazing hot afternoon, with their feet tucked under them.

Some insects are extraordinarily sensitive to temperature. Bees cannot walk when the temperature is below 7°C, cannot fly below 10°C and do not emerge from the hive at temperatures less than 20°C. Grasshoppers cannot jump below 4°C, cannot fly below 8°C and can sing only above 16°C. It is possible to estimate the approximate temperature of the night air by counting the number of chirrups a cricket makes in the space of 14 seconds, then add 40 and you have the correct temperature in Fahrenheit. (To convert to Celsius: F = 9 over 5 + 32.)

I noted one day that a small tree common on our hillsides had a damp patch underneath it. Since no rain had fallen for many hot dry months I was surprised. The tree's common name is *huilboom* or weeping wattle and its Latin name is not difficult to remember, *Peltoforum africanum*, 'the rain is pelting down on the African forum'. When I parked my car under a *Lonchocarpus capassa* and found on my return that, with a perfectly clear sky overhead, I had to turn my windscreen wipers on, I examined the tree more closely. The branches were covered with a multitude of tiny bugs wading around in foamy bubbles of 'cuckoo-spit'. Called froghoppers or spittlebugs (*Ptyelus grossus*), these insects suck the sap from the plant, which, having little nutriment in a lot of liquid, passes through the bug in copious quantities.

I am not alone in my observations. In *African World* of December 1954 an article by Greta Falk tells of the Weeping Rain tree. 'In Main Street, Bulawayo, Southern Rhodesia [now Zimbabwe], amongst jacarandas and silver oaks planted at regular intervals by the Municipality, is one tree protected by railings – an indigenous one known to the Matabele, who are the dominant tribe in these parts, as the 'citamuzi' or rain tree. It is said to revenge itself on anyone who mutilates it. At the beginning of some rainy seasons moisture drips from the leaves of a few isolated specimens of these and runs down the trunk so copiously that the ground around is saturated. Some authorities claim that the phenomenon is caused by a minute insect, *Ptyelus grossus*, others that it is a kind of perspiration. The weeping is an unlucky omen to anyone living in this vicinity, and to build a home of the timber of the 'citamuzi' tree is considered by Africans the height of folly.'

Just to the north of Lulu Phezulu, in the misty forests of Duiwelskloof, lives the Rain Queen. Since the first queen, Dzugudini, ventured south in *c.* 1600 from

Seventeen

Zimbabwe and settled amongst the rare Modjadji cycads (*Encephalartos transvenosus*), the ruling Rain Queen's reputation has spread far and wide. It is not difficult to predict rain if one just watches the leaves of the cycads. During the dry winter weeks the leaves hang down, limp and pale, but when the moisture-laden mists swirl through their prickly branches, the leaves perk up and the Rain Queen pronounces the Coming of the Rain. So accurate is she in her prediction that her power has protected her subjects from invasion by Zulu hordes for centuries, threatening to send drought, disease and locusts to the enemy. The fact that the enemy lives in areas where these natural disasters are not, under normal circumstances, uncommon, only serves to enhance her powers. So, to this day, the Rain Queen rules, the cycads are protected and the rain keeps falling in the tropical forests of Duiwelskloof.

There is a group of plants which has a sensitivity towards external stimuli akin to neurosis. The Brazilian *Mimosa pudica*, which has leaves like an Acacia, has specialised cells at the base of the leaflets which collapse if touched. In fact a loud noise or shout will cause the leaves to wilt suddenly. The swollen base of each leaf stalk microscopically jettisons water by osmosis, causing the leaves to collapse and close in about three seconds, recovering and fleshing out again in sixteen minutes.

The Solomon Islanders can reputedly kill trees by creeping up on them at dawn and suddenly uttering piercing yells close to the trunk. The tree is supposed to die a month later. Our indigenous *Berberis* is also noise-sensitive but I haven't had the heart to creep up on one and yell at it.

Some Acacias close their leaflets at night as if sleeping. But the unfortunate Venus Fly Trap has a mere one second response to any touching and only recovers in twenty-four hours.

Those in touch with their natural surroundings, the country people and the sailors, are full of wisdom about the weather and heed the signs that announce the changes. Townsfolk have to rely on their rheumatism.

If rain is due within twenty-four hours, then bees shelter in their hives, ducks search for snails, garden spiders spin short threads, frogs croak in the daytime, ants hurry about their business, and gnats and mosquitoes fly about in small circles. But probably the sheep are the most sensitive weather forecasters of all. When sheep graze aimlessly there will be no change for days. If a flock is seen moving purposefully in one direction, the wind will come from that direction. Sheep move into the lee of the hills before a gale, and turn their backs against the rain about to fall.

Along the coast of the Western Cape, cocks crowing in the early evening announce misty morning, no matter how clear the evening sky may be. And if gulls fly inland, heavy weather is on the way.

It is well known that just before a storm, swallows swoop low. The airborne insects upon which they prey are forced down by an increase in atmospheric pressure.

Just before rain stopped play in the cricket match at Lord's in 1936, a low-flying cricket-eating sparrow was killed by a ball delivered by Jehangir Khan of Cambridge

Moon halo

University to T.N. Pearce (MCC). The stuffed bird is now on display in a glass case in the clubhouse.

Whilst ostriches actually dance before the rain, horses and mules manage a light-hearted gambol, usually with their tails up in the air.

Although the moon has no actual influence over the weather (that is the sun's pre-rogative), it does tell you what's going to happen. A moon halo means misty weather, while a more defined ring will bring a gale. In the Richtersveld, a distinct halo on two successive nights, and around the sun the following day, preceded a wind so strong that it wrenched my tent from the ground and forced me to take shelter in the vehicle.

A golden full moon warns that rain is near, while a red full moon signals fine, settled weather. If the crescent moon appears with its horns upwards, then it is 'holding the water' and there will be no rain.

Once, as I lay on my back on the cool grass, holding the binoculars steadily over my eyes, I imagined thousands of people doing the same thing, marvelling at a magical moon. It has been, for thousands, maybe millions of years, a romantic shining sphere suspended in a jet black sky. I thought of the ancients trying to understand its phases, its markings, its mysteries. I thought of the astronauts, the scientists, discovering its secrets; its cold silent surface, always the same, always predictable. But as I watched, the familiar round white shape was sucked in by the blackness around it until only the upper left side was lit up. My moon had become a deep orange glow. There was slight atmospheric interference that night, causing the intensity of light to fluctuate, so that it seemed to pulsate with an inner force. In my reverie I began to hallucinate. What a fitting end for mankind if, as we all marvelled at the wonder of the eclipse, staring upwards into a heavenly night, the moon in all its glory were to explode. A gigantic fireworks display, a shower of brilliant white stars, filling the sky with splendour. A fantastic Fourth of July. My birthday. A cataclysmic phenomenon to bring an end to Man's puny existence. I grabbed my binoculars and dived for cover.

The Ground Hornbill

The Ground Hornbill (*Bucorvus leadbeateri*) is now classified as a Red Data species and is protected by law. In times gone by it was used to break the drought. Place one,

dead or alive, in a dry riverbed, and miraculously the river would come down in flood. To find an explanation for this miracle, we have to turn to our biology books. Like those of other hornbills the nest is usually a hole in a tree and, although it is the only hornbill that does not stay completely sealed up, the female does remain on eggs during incubation, a period of forty days and forty nights, during which time it is continually being fed by the male and others within the family group. While she is incarcerated she has to squirt her droppings as far as possible out of a side door. However fastidious and accurate she may be, she is bound to become a little smelly. Austin Roberts's explanation was that 'the bird has so offensive a smell that it will pollute the river, and the river's only hope of getting rid of the foul water is by rising in flood which requires a downpour of rain'.

The Hamerkop

The Hamerkop, or *uthekwane* as it is known to the Zulus, perched for hours on a rock in the river, is thought to be woefully examining himself in the water. 'I am pretty on this side [looking at its face], I am ugly on this side [looking at the back of its head], I am quite spoiled by this affair [referring to its crest], but would that I were wholly pretty.'

Such an interpretation is nonsense: the bird is merely catching its lunch.

The Hamerkop is thought to be a wizard stashing his bewitching bits in the tuft on top of his head. Its habit of conveying to his nest material such as human hair, feathers and wool, thought to be stolen from someone to whom he means harm, often results in the bird being hunted and killed and its nest destroyed. But *uthekwane*, the dull brown one, will take vengeance on anyone demolishing its nest. Great thunderstorms will occur that very day. Furthermore, it will hover over the person found annihilating its nest and defecate on his head, thus pronouncing instant death. An ill-fated journey is predicted when a Hamerkop flies across one's path; so turning back and staying at home for the day is advised. Should anyone throw sticks at *uthekwane* and it dies, they will lose all their hair. It is also said that if this bird is assaulted without actually dying, the assailant will be the one to die.

What is clear from all this is that the Hamerkop is not to be harassed.

It tells us when it is going to rain by uttering a peculiar reedy call interpreted as, 'It's dry! It's dry! The ground is hard!'

Is it not a coincidence that the monotonous croak which is the mating call occurs with the onset of the rainy season, and the collecting of nesting material coincides with the occurrence of thunderstorms?

Nevertheless, a lonely sentinel of dread is the Hamerkop, placed as it is in one genus with only one species – *Scopus umbretta.*

The nest is, however, an architectural marvel. The huge construction is built by both male and female in the fork of a suitable tree, using twigs and leaves. According to Wilson and Wilson, who conducted a survey in central Mali of 180 Hamerkop nests, some bizarre items were included in the later stages of building, such as barbed wire, empty tins, plastic bags, matchboxes, dog excrement, animal bones and balls of wool. A piece of blue cloth was almost always present. The nest is referred to as *efukufukwini,* 'at the rubbish heap'.

The supposition that the nest contains three chambers and that the entrance always faces east is merely folklore and without foundation. In fact, the 90 kg domed structure consists of a sloping passage leading from a mud-lined entrance, inaccessible to predators, to the internal chamber, which provides accommodation for two adults and four or five fully grown young.

A bird with an instinctive memory that it does not need any more, but uses just the same, is the Red-headed Finch, *Amadina erythrocephala.* It is a nest parasite, which uses the nests of other birds such as sparrows and weavers, and no longer builds its own. When sitting on a nest, however, the bird still performs all the nest-building movements, but in a random sequence. It reaches over the edge of the nest and 'grasps' and pulls in the non-existent nest material as if it were actually building.

A certain species of New Zealand moth emerges from its chrysalis just a few hours before the approach of low-pressure cold fronts bringing rain. Experiments were conducted and it was surmised that the ratios of positive to negative atmospheric ions might be the 'trigger' for the moth's emergence.

The Gaudy Commodore, *Junonia octavia sesamus*, must surely be one of nature's most imaginative butterflies. In a wet summer the male Gaudy Commodore appears from his pupa with salmon-pink wings, but in winter, when no rain falls, they will be a violet-blue.

Also duping us into believing that it is two separate species is the Club-tailed Emperor, *Charaxes zoolina zoolina*, appearing in summer with greenish-white wings and in winter with orange-brown wings.

If you thought that the difference between a tortoise and a turtle is that a turtle lives in water, you would be right most of the time, except in spring, just before the first rains. When the hot dry August wind blows across the parched plains of the Karoo and Namaqualand, the resident tortoises, called the Karoo Padlopers (*Homopus boulengeri*), seek out the last remaining puddles of water and float there like small patterned islands. As weather forecasters, tortoises fare well and are a good buy. Every farmer should have one. As indicators of when to sow seed, they are second only to the Agricultural Officer, who may not be available and may sometimes be wrong. There may be not a cloud in the sky when the tortoises start their perambulations and are encountered in fairly good numbers crossing roads (hence their name *padlopers*) in their determination to reach higher ground. Between twelve and twenty-four hours later, thunderclouds will gather and rain will fall (hence their Afrikaans names *donderweerskilpad*, *reënskilpad*, *swaarweerskilpad* and *onweerskilpad*).

Archie's father kept tortoises in a large enclosure and declared that his tortoises always walked downhill if there was going to be a dry spell and uphill if rain was due, their sixth sense warning them to avoid the inevitable flash floods so characteristic of desert rainstorms. Not only that, but, if after his long winter hibernation, the tortoise wakes up to warm weather, he will not eat a leaf until the last cold snap has passed. And if you see a female laying her eggs, make a note of the date because

The Gaudy Commodore, Junonia octavia sesamus, *must surely be one of nature's most imaginative butterflies. In a wet summer the male Gaudy Commodore appears from his pupa with salmon-pink wings, but in winter, when no rain falls, they will be a violet-blue.*

Also duping us into believing that it is two separate species is the Club-tailed Emperor, Charaxes zoolina zoolina, *appearing in summer with greenish-white wings and in winter with orange-brown wings.*

spring will begin exactly thirteen months later.

A terrapin is neither a turtle nor a tortoise but pretends it's a lion. Like most potential victims when threatened, the terrapin emits a powerful and offensive odour which smells like lions, thus frightening off most predators. The blood of terrapins is regarded by some African people as a remedy for fits.

Farmers in the Bushveld can tell whether it will be a good rainy season or not. When the Spotted-backed Weavers choose to hang their nests from the lowest branches overhanging the rivers or dams, no rains can be expected, since little change in the water level is predicted. But when the nests are tied to the upper branches, good rains in the distant catchment areas are promised.

I am told that when it's going to rain, peacock feathers, which are normally green, turn blue.

~

The earth's magnetic pull plays an essential role in the direction-finding system of many creatures. It certainly does in the migration of robins, seals, fish and mice. Professor Günter Becker received a boxful of Zimbabwean termite queens with which to experiment. In the evening he shook them onto the bottom of a breeding box, where they lay in all directions. The next morning he saw to his astonishment that they had, without exception, all settled down to sleep lying in an east–west position. The professor cautiously turned the box 90 degrees, but after a few hours the insects had corrected their positions so that their heads were either east or west.

I've always believed one should sleep with one's head facing north. Architects designing houses should plan for the foot of the bed not to be positioned facing the door. Only corpses lie like that. They should also make sure that the bed is placed lying the same way as the floorboards and in sympathy with the other woodwork of the chamber, for if it is placed across the boards of the

floor it will prevent sleep or, worse, a dying man lying under the cross-beam of a house will pass away in pain.

It all boils down to being in harmony with one's surroundings.

To get out of bed on the right side is vital to ensure a lucky day. Does that mean not the left side, or not the wrong side? The original formulators of these superstitions obligingly leave one's options open.

If domesticated ostriches escape from a paddock they always travel north. In their paddocks some mysterious attraction directs them to the northern fence along which they pace restlessly, up and down, for hours.

In times gone by, if a wild ostrich was caught by a tribesman it had to be taken to the chief, who accepted the feathers and any eggs that were found, but the hunter was allowed to keep the meat. In return the hunter was also given a goat.

The male ostrich shares in the task of incubating the eggs. Being black and therefore invisible at night he takes the night shift, while the female, whose drab brown coloration blends with the surrounding bush, sits on the eggs during the day. She, of course, is protecting the eggs from the direct rays of the sun, whilst at night the temperature of the eggs has to be kept at 34°C for them to hatch.

Before they hatch, an ostrich egg, scrambled, is equivalent to 24 hens' eggs. Serve on toast with a bottle of bubbly. (To retain the fizz in a half-finished bottle of champagne, place a spoon, handle down, into the neck of the bottle, and it will last for a week in the fridge.)

Doreen tells me that putting a wilted lettuce in a bowl of water with a silver fork makes the lettuce fresh and crisp again.

> Is it the size of the tines,
> the time of the signs,
> the sign of the times?

All living things have an energy and Doreen's lettuce leaves are no exception. It is an electric field, a life force, an aura, call it what you will, and it has been photographed.

In 1941, in Krasnodar in the Soviet Union, Semyon Davidovich Kirlian, electrician

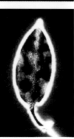

Electro-magnetic photographs of a thumbprint and leaves

and amateur photographer, and his wife Valentina devised a method of recording luminescence. By laying film in contact with an object to be photographed and passing light through the object from a high-frequency spark generator, the Kirlians had come across a way of photographing a phenomenon which has captured the imagination of scientists throughout the world. If the leaf they were photographing was fresh, then white, blue and even red and yellow flares were pictured surging out of what seemed to be channels in the leaves. These emanations, or force fields round a leaf, became distorted if the leaf was mutilated, gradually diminishing and disappearing as the leaf was allowed to die. Even Doreen's fork would then have no effect.

The Kirlians continued to work on their experiments, magnifying their photographic processes to optical instruments and microscopes, allowing this energy to be seen as 'whirling fireballs, starry points of light and miniature volcanoes'. However, things were slow to catch fire in scientific circles in the Soviet Union at that time and it was another ten years before the Kirlians emerged from obscurity.

In the early 1960s Dr Lev Fedorov of the USSR's Ministry of Public Health awarded the Kirlians their first research grant, that they might pursue their photography and apply it to medical diagnoses. However, when Dr Fedorov died soon thereafter, official funding from Moscow began to dwindle and the academic sceptics and bureaucrats were once more in control. It was not until the spring of 1972 that the first Western conference on Kirlian Photography and the Human Aura was held at Manhattan's United Engineering Center, where a crowd of doctors, psychiatrists, psychologists, parapsychologists, biologists, engineers and photographers packed the auditorium to capacity.

A year later a second meeting was held in New York's Town Hall. Dr John Pierrakos, a Greek-born psychiatrist, stated publicly that he used his unusual heightened perceptions of the human aura to assist him in his diagnoses. 'Man is an eternal pendulum of movement and vibration,' he told the Town Hall audience. 'His spirit is captured in a body in which forces throb and pulsate like the beat of a heart. Often they thunder and quake in his body with strong emotions that shake the very foundations of his physical being. Life goes on, rhythmically and quietly pulsating with the warm feeling of love or cascading with avalanches of violent emotion, for movement and pulsation is life. When movement diminishes, the person becomes ill, and when movement stops, the person is dying.'

Pierrakos showed detailed drawings of auras which he could visually perceive around plants, animals and human beings and which he was able to monitor in continual movement around neurotically and psychotically disturbed patients. In his pictures he illustrated the three layers he sees around most of his patients. The first, a dark band, no more than one-sixteenth to one-eighth of an inch thick, lies close to the skin and looks like a transparent crystalline structure. The second, a broader dark-blue layer, reminiscent of a cluster of iron filings, forms an ovoid envelope around the body when seen from the front. The third is a lightish-blue haze of radiant energy which, when the patient is in good health, extends several feet away from the body and accounts for why we describe zestful persons as 'radiant'.

It is strange, though, that the points where the Kirlian lights flashed most brilliantly on the human body appeared to match the acupuncture points mapped by the Chinese. But still it is the domain of the faith healers, quacks and clairvoyants, unproven and searching for significant recognition.

One thing, however, is certain, and all gamblers will concur, that every number has a certain potency in symbolism, some more than others.

SEVEN takes the cake.

It is the number of days in a week, the number of candles in a Hebrew candelabrum, there are seven heavens, seven hells, seven veils, seven major planets, seven metals, seven Ages of Man, seven pillars of wisdom, seven notes of the scale, seven seas, seven deadly sins,* seven wonders of the world and seven colours of the rainbow. The seven-year itch is the period beyond which any married couple can reasonably be expected to stay together. The seventh son to be born is always lucky or an especially gifted person, often blessed with occult powers. He makes a good doctor and usually has an instinctive knowledge of magic and medicinal herbs.

The flowers of the *Helichrysum* family, the *sewejaartjie* or 'everlasting', are believed to last for seven years. They are used for wreaths and dried-flower arrangements, but on no account should the plant be ripped out of the earth with its roots. It should be

* Lust, Avarice, Sloth, Wrath, Pride, Envy, Gluttony

approached so that your shadow falls over it, preferably picked in the very early morning before dawn 'when there are no shadows', or in the very late evening, after sunset. Furthermore, because the plant is believed to be like the shades, and should be respected, great care must be taken not to look into the earth when breaking off the flowers. 'To look there is to look at a shade. This is not done. A man must not look at his fathers.'

There are over 200 varieties of this plant, nearly all with a good strong colour and a sweet smell which, once smelt, cannot be forgotten or confused with other odours.

'Inhaling the smoke of a burning *imphepho* (*Helichrysum nudifolium*) bush gives us a remembering mind. It is given to us by the shades so that we may forget nothing.' If you consider smoke inhalation harmful to your health, rather place *imphepho* under your pillow. It has the same effect and has the added advantage of clearing your dreams, curing your colds or relieving your hiccups.

Man can distinguish 250 pure colours, from red through orange to yellow, through green to blue and indigo, up to violet, and about 17 000 mixed colours, plus about 300 shades of grey between black and white. So mixing and multiplying all those together,

we can see about 5 million shades of colour, as compared with a bee, which, in spite of its 15 000 eye facets, can see only 12 colours and red not at all. How do we know? A simple experiment with bees was conducted as follows.

Small squares of grey paper of different shades but equal brightness were set like the squares of a chessboard, and one blue square was included in the middle. Each square was fitted with a tiny dish, but the blue square's dish had syrup in it. After lengthy trials a bee could be taught to fly straight to the blue square, even when its position was moved about on the board. Yet, when a red paper of equal brightness replaced the blue, the bee was flummoxed, and could not tell it from the grey. Bees must therefore be blind to red. A bee's vision has its own basic colours of green, purple, blue, yellow and ultraviolet, the last of which is invisible to us. Blue and yellow flowers are particularly attractive to bees, while reds attract butterflies and birds.

House-flies see blue, and dislike it enough to avoid blue-hued windows or blue walls and curtains, while mosquitoes, which are known to distinguish yellow, white and black, appear to prefer black. In an experiment in an insect-infested region in Oregon, seven men wore shirts of different colours. Within half a minute the black shirt had attracted most insects: 1499 compared with only 520 on the shirt next most infected, a white one.

I have it on good authority, and to a certain extent on personal experience, that to deter the tsetse fly in the Okavango Swamps one should wear a pale blue shirt and a sickly-sweet, heavily perfumed deodorant. In fact, the less you look and smell like a warthog, the better.

In days gone by, when young Zulu men left home to work on farms and distant towns, they had no knowledge of writing, so messages were conveyed between lovers in the 'language of beads', the Zulu love letter (*incwadi kuthanda*). Tiny glass beads, which came originally from Czechoslovakia, found their way into Zululand via the Portuguese traders in Delagoa Bay. Initially, a single strand of twine was threaded through different-coloured beads, and the meaning interpreted from one end to the other, but later whole letters evolved, taking the shape of an ornamental square, the 'message' being read from the outer edge towards the centre.

A simplified 'dictionary' of colours developed, the meanings of which are derived

from nature. Some of the colours and interpretations may vary from area to area but generally the message will be unmistakable if the following colours are used:

White (*thambo* / bone) – represents purity, cleanliness, true love and hope.

Black (*sitimane* / shadow) – shows grief, loneliness, disappointment ('My heart has become as black as the rafters on the roof, as I hear you have another maiden').

Red (*igazi* / blood) – indicates intense love, longing ('My heart bleeds for you').

Ruby (*umlilwane* / flames) – She burns with love, as the flames of a grass fire.

Yellow (*incombo* / young corn) – represents wealth (or lack of it!).

Green (*ukuhlaza* / new grass) – implies love-sickness, jealousy ('I have become as thin as a blade of new grass from pining for you').

Blue (*ijuba* / dove) – symbolises faithfulness, also calmness and cleanliness, as clear as the blue sky ('If I were a dove, I would fly the endless skies to you').

Light turquoise (*ifefe* / pigeon) – He talks too much, and cannot keep a secret!

Dark turquoise (*ijubatondo* / pigeon) – shows impatience ('I am losing hope that you will ever marry me').

Pink (*siphofu* / poor one) – signifies abject poverty. She doubts he will ever afford to pay her *lobola* (bride price, paid in cattle).

Purple (*obu-khuwebezane*) – new friendship.

Brown (*nhlabathi* / soil) – My love is like the earth, which gives rise to new life.

Striped beads (*ntothoviyane* / striped grasshopper) – implies doubt, or accusations of fickleness, or two-timing ('You are like *ntothoviyane*, springing from bush to bush').

We all know that black absorbs heat and white reflects, so it would seem that black is not a sensible colour to wear in the desert, yet the Bedouin of the Negev, where temperatures may reach 46°C, wear loose black garments with no apparent discomfort. Amiram Shkolnick, of Tel Aviv University, found that in the midday sun the black robes had a surface temperature 6°C higher than that of the white robes, yet the skin

Chameleon

temperature of each wearer was the same, 33°C. The temperature of the air between the skin and the outer garment, whether white or black, was the same, 38°C. 'It seems that convection of heat occurs either by air flow from the base of the loose garment as the wearer moves, or as a result of the so-called chimney effect of the air space between the robes and the skin. Thus the greater convection of air generated by black robes might make them more comfortable to wear than white garments.' Besides, Bedouin apparel is black because it is woven from the wool of black goats.

To give an uneven number of flowers in a bunch is considered in Russia to be unlucky. It is unlucky to give white flowers to sick people, the implication being that they would be more suitable for a funeral. Red roses, particularly full-blown ones, are also considered unlucky. Red and white flowers together are omens of death. Adding another colour to the arrangement makes them acceptable.

If you are now totally confused, spare a thought for the chameleon, whose eyes act independently of one another, or that colourful duck the Mallard, *Anas platyrhynchos*, which enjoys a panoramic view of its surroundings. Graham Martin of the University of Birmingham investigated the scope of vision using an ophthalmoscope. The device directs a beam of light into the subject's eye along the line of sight of the observer, who sees a reflection from the subject's retina. To survey an animal's visual field, the observer simply moves around the immobilised creature and notes the point at which light is no longer reflected. Martin's results reveal that the Mallard's visual field completely encircles its head, thereby enabling it to detect predators approaching from any quarter. This must be the only advantage considering that in most birds the eyes weigh more than the brain.

Dassies are able to detect the approach of a predator a kilometre away, and since their main concern is attack from the sky they sunbathe with their eyes open, being able to gaze directly into the sun. This has led to the belief that they are blind. In fact, their eye possesses a special membrane, the umbraculum, which protects the retina and allows light to penetrate only at the sides of the pupil. It is thus possible to detect a Black Eagle against the sun without damage to the retina.

Observe young children being introduced to each other. Like dogs sniffing in greeting, children will display curiosity, suspicion and reticence. They will never smile. It is an honest appraisal, untrammelled by etiquette. By analysing photographs of adults, Irenaus Eibl-Eibesfeldt discovered that when a person meets someone he likes and trusts, both his eyebrows shoot up for about one-sixth of a second. This response is instantaneous and completely unconscious.

When the other person, also unconsciously, observes someone twitch his eyebrow, he is likely to think, 'My, what a nice person!' and the meeting will get off to a good start.

Watching the behaviour of things can, however, be misinterpreted.

The Red-throated Wryneck, *Jynx ruficollis*, is unique in its behaviour and therefore has attracted the interest of imaginative myth-makers. Firstly, its name, *Jynx*, suggests that it puts a jinx on ants, and many stories abound connecting the two. One fanciful story, of its lying down near an ants' nest, pretending to be dead and letting the ants creep into its mouth, is related without the benefit of the knowledge that an anatom-

The Red-throated Wryneck

ical aberration allows the wryneck to turn its head right round over its shoulder, making it appear as if it were dead or hypnotising the ants. This unusual behaviour gives rise to yet another story. It is believed to be able to restore the affections of a wayward lover, although how this is accomplished I do not know, except perhaps by 'turning the other cheek', or 'turning a blind eye'.

The only role, apart from cleaning up the place, as far as I can see, for the little brown ant is that of providing for the birds some form of bizarre entertainment. To watch a bird lying on the ground, wings outstretched, can mean one of two things. It is either sunbathing or anting. If the bird is lying on or near an ants' nest, picking up ants in its beak and rubbing them along the underside of its wings, it could be simply allowing the ants to bite off any lice under the wingpits, but the look of ecstasy and its trance-like state could be exposing antics of a more kinky kind.

James Clarke says that birds will use substitutes such as wasps – even cigarette ends, onions and smoke – and the sessions can last up to one hour. Large birds have been observed sitting over burning tufts of grass for several seconds at a time. The flight of the Phoenix could simply have been a frantic search for water to douse his flaming feathers after indulging in foolish perversions.

If you see an ant or a whole kibbutz of ants, you can safely bet that it or they will be female. The few males live deep in the nest and their only function is to mate, after which they die. None ever reaches the status of king.

On a patch of bare soil near a termite heap next to the *Cussonia* graveyard someone had spilled a crate of popcorn. Well, that's what Max said. On investigation I found countless thousands of tiny white mushrooms. On further investigation I identified them as *Termitomyces microcarpus*, and learnt that they grow in association with highly enterprising termites.

If our human society could be as efficient as that of the termite, *we* would inherit the earth, but it seems that at the rate we're going *they* ultimately shall have dominion.

Termites should not be called white ants; they are, in fact, very different from ants. Apart from physical differences their ancestry goes back one hundred million years; their social life is more sophisticated than the ants'; and there are more of them.

Living as they do in complicated termite heaps, which require building, repairing,

cleaning and ventilating, most members of the colony grow up to be workers – soft-bodied, slow-moving, blind workers. Unlike ants they can be either male or female. A mere five per cent of the colony are soldiers with huge jaws that offer a pugnacious response to any attack by intruders. When the workers are out foraging for food, a few soldiers will accompany them, purely for protection; *en route* they will be fed by the workers. The worker swallows a piece of food and may pass some or all of his partially

Max and friend

digested meal to any passerby who may be hungry. Nothing is ever wasted. A meal can pass a few times through many individuals until nothing but a brown paste remains, with which the last to leave the table fixes a crack in the wall. All corpses are also eaten.

The termite heap itself is a functional living entity comparable architecturally to the Great Pyramid of Egypt.

It is constantly being irrigated and incubated.

The worker termites collect fungus spores whilst gathering dry timber, twigs and leaf mould. These are chewed, regurgitated and formed into a spongy cellular comb. Kept damp, the spores ripen and grow into mushrooms, thereby raising the temperature in the termite heap and providing the young termites with warmth and food. Deep in the centre of this extraordinary construction lives the queen, a bloated, lumpy, egg-laying machine, up to 10 cm in length, pampered by the workers and serviced periodically by her timid king, who spends his off-duty time cowering in the corner.

One more case where being male in the insect world is no fun.

~

My dislike for the little brown Argentinian ant is completely forgotten when I consider the Cheetah. In her book *Cheetah under the Sun*, Nan Wrogeman pleads for the preservation of the Cheetah, 'a creature so regal and aloof, so beautiful and lithe, in movement a symphony of natural grace'.

~

What constitutes Beauty? Hardy said, 'Beauty lies not in the thing, but in what the thing symbolised.' So, it is no wonder that we see no beauty in the bat. They hang upside down, which is absurd, they inhabit unsavoury places, like abandoned buildings and caves; they are nocturnal, promiscuous and sometimes cannibalistic. But they do have one remarkable attribute. The 'bashed in' look to their noses is because of, and not in spite of, their remarkable navigation system. They can fly about in the dark without smashing into anything, which makes them more respectable than, say, a rose beetle. They send out pulsating sounds, which are sometimes of such a high pitch as to be beyond the threshold of human audibility. Some bats in flight can detect and avoid

Cheetah

wires only 0.1 mm thin. So they will never, never blunder into anything. 'As blind as a bat' is a total myth: they can see well in broad daylight and very well at night.

We had one which lived on the lintel above the front door, upside down, of course. We called him Hildebrand, and apart from creating a sticky patch on the floor every morning, he caused us no trouble; in fact, the way he tilted his head this way and that to watch us as we passed underneath was quite endearing.

A thought has crossed my mind. Surely it's rather inconvenient, not to say unhygienic, to defecate upside down?

That bats fly in the dark is ascribed by Aesop to their avoidance of creditors, or by the Yavapai Indians of Arizona as a search for wives who ran away when they saw the bats in the light. A Chinese legend has it that the bat flies head downward because its brains are so heavy.

In parts of Australia, in Bosnia and in Shropshire, England, bats are respected, as they purportedly contain the souls of the dead, and are never killed. By the way, anyone with a bat phobia is called a chiropterophobe.

A bat coming into the house is an indicator of death according to folk beliefs recorded in India, Alabama and Salzburg, whilst in China and Poland it is a good sign, signifying long life and happiness. The Zulus will not touch a bat, but in Mississippi a heart cut from a live bat and tied to the wrist where it cannot be seen brings luck at the gambling tables.

There is a widespread belief that bats will become entangled in women's hair and that a bat can cling to a person's face.

One warm October evening when we were all in the sitting-room, my mother-in-law, an infrequent visitor and terrified of everything that flies, crawls or scurries, was sitting in a chair in the centre of the room. A bat flew in. I was quick to try to assure her of her absolute safety, that the bat would not trouble her, and proceeded to explain its infallible echo-location abilities. My future credibility as a purveyor of scientific information was destroyed, when Peter's Epauletted Bat flew straight towards her and landed on

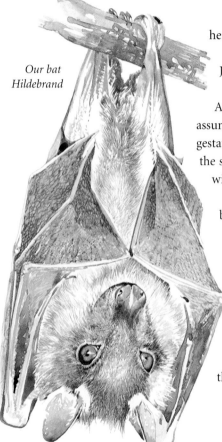

*Our bat
Hildebrand*

her lap. Its behaviour to this day remains inexplicable and condemned.

The first specimen to be found of the rare Lesueur's Hairy Bat was named after J.S. LeSueur, whe rescued it from his cat.

In most insectivorous bats it was found that copulation took place in mid-April but that ovulation and fertilisation occurred only in mid-September. It was assumed that the females stored the sperm in their uterine horns during winter. The gestation period was estimated to be 63 days in the case of a Temminck's Hairy Bat, the singletons being born from late October to the middle of November to coincide with the warm wet months of the year when insects are freely available.

In China, if you want to wish someone well, you send him a present with two bats drawn on the wrapping.

In the period between 1967 and 1977 there were several hundred reports in America of bats which had attacked people without warning or provocation. On 15 June 1964, at the New York World's Fair, at 2.30 p.m., a seven-year-old boy and his mother were leaving the fairgrounds when a bat swooped down, out of nowhere, collided with the boy, and bit him. Both the boy and his mother were tested for rabies and found to be negative. The only explanation given was that the increase in the use of insecticides had increased the toxicity of the insects on which the bats feed. This in turn had attacked the nervous system of the bat, enough to disorientate and derange him completely.

I wish I could tell my mother-in-law.

chapter eight

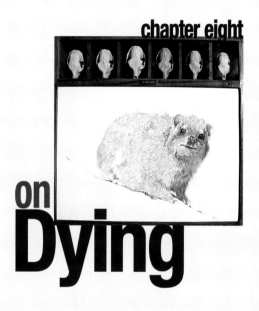

on Dying

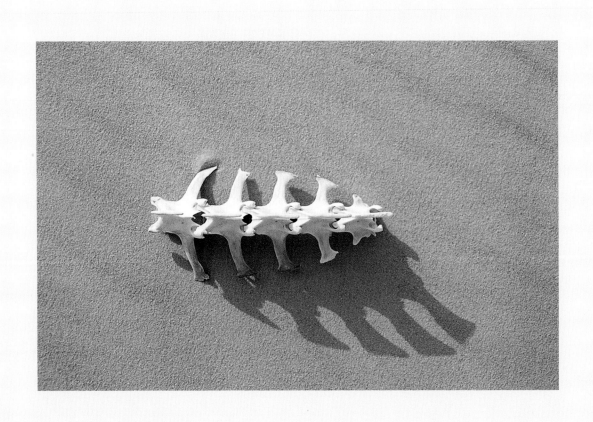

W E HAD A NEUROTIC DOG called Nigel. Always a free spirit and brave to the marrow, he chased baboons, Bushbuck and Bushpigs, and was unafraid of Porcupines, but he could not handle a collar. He was six years old when we had reason to collar him for the first time. We had taken him to the city and wanted to walk him where other dogs walked. The rules of the recreation park required that all dogs be on a lead. I bought a simple leather collar and metal chain, and slipped it gently round his neck. He stood immobilised, wouldn't budge. Dogaleptic. I thought that after a few times he would get used to it. To the day he died, Nigel could not wear a collar without going into a resolute motionless trance.

We bought a cat. Victor was a pale-cream Siamese and he ruled our lives. Poor Victor was only seven months old when a temporary wooden shelf fell and killed him. We were very sad and gave him a proper funeral with music and flowers. Max and Walter made a graveyard under a large *Cussonia spicata* on the koppie behind the house. All their deceased beetles, birds and Emperor Moths were buried there, according to status, each with appropriately sized wooden cross- es so that God knew where they were. Before laying him to rest, I had considered painting Victor's lifeless body, as I had painted the limp birds and mice that he had presented to me in his short lifetime, but the children wouldn't let me. Later on we had two Siamese cats, a mother and daughter, who were to be seen constantly together in book-end positions, mirror images or double visions.

I was one of those human mothers who shied away from unmentionable subjects like the death of the children's favourite silkworm or frog. The passing of a pet was a tragedy in our house. I used to hide the lifeless bodies and would tell the children they'd gone to Jesus. One day, after the fifteenth frog went missing, Walter said in a puzzled and thoughtful way, 'Jesus must have a lot of dead things.'

It was time to tell him the truth.

Most of the things that I painted ran or crawled or flew away. My specimens from the freezer, like the Wahlberg's Epauletted Bat a friend gave me, would thaw and leak all over the page while being painted.

Our two Siamese cats, a mother and daughter, were to be seen constantly together in book-end positions, mirror images or double visions.

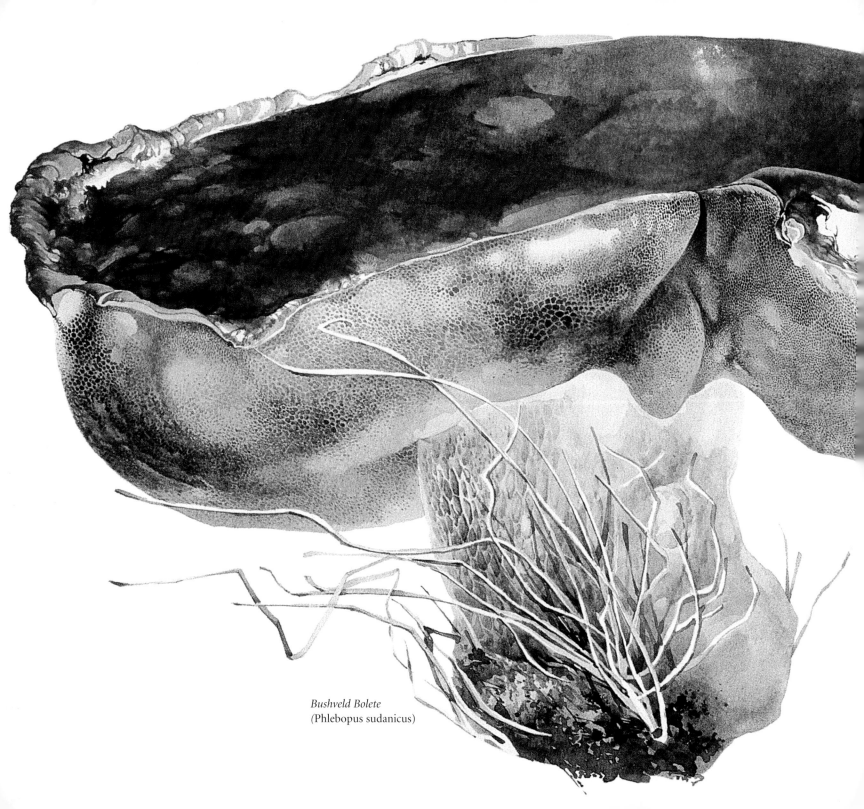

Bushveld Bolete
(Phlebopus sudanicus)

I was once halfway through a painting of a Bushveld Bolete mushroom, a really large one, 40 cm across. Overnight and without warning it collapsed into a liquid mass of tiny crawling maggots making thousands of delicate dark trails all over the paper.

Mushrooms can also dissolve, unaided by maggots, into a liquid mess. The candle-shaped Shaggy Ink Cap, *Coprinus comatus*, deliquesces into an excellent permanent black ink, and depending on your needs of the moment you can either write with it or eat it. This mushroom, picked during its pristine prime, is delicious. Save the older ones for ink.

Donald Culross Peattie once said, 'Fungi are the clandestine underworld of the plant kingdom, taking cover in unfavourable times, rioting in others.'

Anyone who has suffered anything from athlete's foot to rotten floorboards will know the insidious nature of fungus, scavenging, parasitising. Circles of lush darker green grass on the lawn or in a pasture, usually with an enclosed bare zone of compacted soil, indicate the presence of a fungus called *Marasmius oreades*. These 'fairy rings' conjure up an image of 'little folk' in a magical play but are, in fact, the visible fruiting part of a larger, living cobweb-like colony under the ground. As the centre dies off, the hyphae or little threads gradually widen out, as in a ripple, waiting for the right temperature and humidity when, suddenly, overnight, toadstools will spring up in a clearly defined circle. Legend says they are caused by a foal being born on that spot or the dancing places of fairies and that it is wrong to interfere with such a place in any way, for to do so will surely strike you blind or lame.

Magic mushrooms have intrigued us all from time to time but mycologist Dr Patrick Harding from Sheffield University has taken the matter a step further. He says that the hallucinogenic properties of the Fly Agaric (*Amanita muscaria*) are responsible for some of the myths surrounding that most hallowed of traditional festivals, Christmas. Santa Claus, dressed in his red and white robes, originates from the frozen forests of Lapland. The Lapp or medicine man, having eaten the mushroom, would twitch and sweat, peeing into the snow as he went. In his trance state, he would have the sensation of flying, taking leave of his body, communicating with the spirits and jumping down chimneys to heal the sick in the village. His reindeer, so Dr Harding informs us, lick the yellow snow, stained by human urine con-

Shaggy Ink Cap (Coprinus comatus)

The Fly Agaric (Amanita muscaria)

taining muscimol, the hallucinogenic property of the red and white Fly Agaric. The reindeer would then also become affected, earning their image of being able to fly across the star-studded sky pulling a sleigh laden with presents. Naturally Santa would vocalise in his euphoric state, so 'ho, ho, ho' seems a plausible enough sound for him to make.

Magic mushrooms also distort the ability to judge size, so anything will appear either very big or very small. This state is called macropsia. Perhaps the authors of Alice in her Wonderland, Jack and his Beanstalk, Gulliver on his Travels and Thumbelina also indulged in the delights of *Amanita muscaria*.

When the early rains brought the first flush of field mushrooms we gathered baskets full. Those we could not eat immediately we cooked and stored in the neighbour's freezer. The tasty, highly sought-after field mushroom *Agaricus campestris* has four spores on each basidium, whereas the cultivated supermarket mushroom *Agaricus bisporus* has only two. Twice the flavour, half the price.

A prize find in the pine forest is the *Boletus badius*; fried in butter it is every bit as good as the better-known Cep (*Boletus edulis*) but has the advantage of seldom being infested with maggots. It is reddish-brown on top, bruises bluish, and the tubes are pale cream when young, then becoming ochre. It has a mild earthy smell. Whilst the Cep likes to disguise itself as a nobble of needles, the Bay, as it is known, stands proud and solitary.

The I'Kowe, *Termitomyces umkowaani*, is an enormous mushroom, dinner-plate size, and quite delicious. It grows tall and erect in lush pastures, always indicating subterranean termite nests. Although it has white gills (one needs to be especially suspicious of anything with white gills) it is very different in character from the deadly *Amanitas*. It has a typical mushroom smell and may cause mild discomfort for some people if eaten raw, but when

Boletus edulis

Agaricus campestris

Parasol Mushrooms

grilled, gill-side up, with a dab of butter and a light sprinkling of salt and pepper, it is absolutely delicious.

In spite of its easily recognisable characteristics, we do pick the Parasol Mushroom, *Macrolepiota zeyheri*, with caution, because it has a poisonous cousin, the False Parasol, *Chlorophyllum molybdites*, which resembles it closely. The False Parasol has a smooth brown skin at the centre of the cap, like a yarmulka, breaking up into little scales, diminishing in number and size towards the edges. The margin is curved and bent inwards and the cap is generally bell-like when mature. The most distinctive feature of this poisonous mushroom is that it has a greenish tinge to the gills and the spore print is green, whereas in the edible parasol both the gills and the spore print are pure white. Once you know the difference, a taste sensation is in store for you.

We learnt to leave well alone those we knew to be poisonous. In fact, we learnt those first and, being optimists, regarded all else as possible meals. The deadly *Amanita phalloides*, or Death Cap, was one to which we paid particular attention, because anything so diabolically dangerous held a morbid fascination for us. Even the spores of this mushroom in a basket full of edible mushrooms render the whole lot suspect and to be thrown out.

The Death Caps grow under exotic trees, such as oaks, poplars and pines, the spores or bits of mycelium having been brought here at the time those trees were introduced. When it first appears above the ground the mushroom is covered entirely with a white membrane, which later tears, exposing the pale green cap. Once it has opened properly the soft fragile ring can be seen attached quite high up on the slender stem. The ring was at first a membrane, stretching from the margin of the cap to the stem. This tears as the fungus grows, leaving an imprint of the gills still showing on the ring with remnants of the ring hanging like frills

The False Parasol

The deadly Amanita phalloides, *or Death Cap*

on the margin of the mushroom. The base of the stem is thick and bulbous, well set in the ground, and covered with a whitish, thick-skinned casing or volva. The phallus part of the name is not what it seems. Before the volva breaks, the fungus looks like a pigeon's egg. Phallus also means egg. It has a characteristic slightly honey-sweet smell, becoming increasingly strong, finally astringent and objectionable. Its greenish tinge should alert even the most careless of hunter-gatherers. The strange thing is that snails can eat the mushroom with no serious ill effects and rabbits are able to tolerate fairly large quantities. This led to the belief that rabbits contain antidotes to the poison. So in the old days someone who had eaten a poisonous mushroom was advised to swallow a mixture of finely chopped rabbit gut and brain, washed down with sugar solution. Another complicated procedure was to filter the patient's blood four times through charcoal granules on an artificial liver machine. Neither treatment was effective. The poison contained in *Amanita phalloides* is merciless and no effective antidote has yet been found. After consuming the mushroom, one experiences no discomfort until at least six hours later, and in some cases as much as forty-eight hours later. Then suddenly the victim experiences intense thirst, abdominal pains, vomiting, cold sweats and diarrhoea. After two days the symptoms subside, only to recur in more intense form. The entire nervous system becomes paralysed, the liver degenerates and the patient slips into a coma accompanied by violent delirium, general collapse and death.

Nasty.

I was once poisoned by the yellow-staining mushroom *Agaricus xanthoderma*. The poison affects one in six people. After three days of vomiting, sweating and stomach pains, it left me with a decided antipathy to all fungi, which I retained for many years. When that disappeared it was replaced by fascination, but I now advocate extreme caution when picking mushrooms from the veld. Once you know the four or five choice species, there is no finer free food.

~

Kalonga – the Creator of all Things – decreed that certain animals are holy and that it is forbidden, under threat of severe punishment, to interfere with or kill them. The fish eagle is Kalonga's voice, heard in the rich sonorous call of this bird, which can only be interpreted by the diviner.

An awesome eagle to be both feared and protected is the Bateleur (*Terathopius ecaudatus*). The cry of the Bateleur is seldom heard, which is fortunate because it indicates that war is imminent. But it has two cries: the short barking cry which is the ominous one, and a prolonged cry which, if heard by someone on a journey, should alert the traveller to take evasive action, for his life is supposedly threatened. The Bateleur had foreseen the danger and warns him of it. If it flies overhead and perchance covers you with its shadow, you will never again have full use of your senses; and worse still, if it throws a mute on a man's head, he will die immediately.

The distant hills with their rugged kloofs and indigenous forests are feeding and breeding grounds for the mighty Crowned Eagle. These majestic birds are fiercely territorial, overseeing a kingdom of many square kilometres.

Walter, passionate about aviation, invested his savings in a radio-controlled model glider kit. It took him a month of Sundays to construct the delicate balsawood frame, cover it with taut white-, yellow-, orange- and red-striped plastic, and decorate it with decals. The receiver in place, the batteries charged, the prized creation was launched into the wind from the summit of Mount Carmel. The valley below was like an aerial photograph and his plucky little plane swooped and looped, soared and roared, dived and climbed. Suddenly, literally out of the blue, came the owner of this vast territory. First, an investigative sortie, then a taunting challenge, then a defiant attack. Walter, struggling to contain his excitement and overcome his dyslexia, managed to avoid the eagle at each turn. When the glider was landed it bore the wounds of talons in its tail, now to be circled in Koki pen and proudly displayed to model aeroplane fanatics.

Wilf is a journalist, always on the look-out for a good story. Most times journalists have to scout for stories, but not Wilf. Not this time, anyway. Late one afternoon Wilf and I were looking for fossils along a dry river bank in the Karoo National Park. As we walked along a sandy riverbed we noticed a Black Eagle circling overhead. They are not

Fish Eagle

Black Eagle

uncommon in the high cliffs, preying on the dassies that sun themselves on the rocks. This one circled lower as if questioning our presence in his territory, his small head tilting curiously from side to side. Suddenly he dived towards the rocky ledge above us and disappeared. We did not see it take off again, so, thinking that it might have caught a dassie, we clambered up to see if we could spot it. As we hauled ourselves up the steepest part we had a good view of the territory beyond. No more than fifty metres away, perched on a rock was the most haughty-looking of all the eagles in Africa. We tried to get a little closer by climbing up the grass-covered slope towards the ridge. Black Eagles can probably spot a dassie two kilometres away and Wilf is not a small man. My gasps of excitement were enough to scare off the most belligerent of beasts. But instead of being scared off it stood its ground. We assumed it had a nest nearby or that it was reluctant to let go of the prey it may have caught. So we crept closer. When we were within thirty metres it suddenly launched itself towards us and swooped down, talons extended. We could hear the rush of wind in its feathers as it came to within inches of our heads, sending us diving for cover into a dense tangle of thornbushes. The bird rose slowly, and landed on a rock a little distance away. Our knees were awash with adrenalin and dripping with blood. A second time it came, and a third. The story growing in Wilf's head for the front page of his newspaper ran out of superlatives:

Famous Newspaperman Felled by Ferocious Eagle.

We later found out that the 'owner' of the eagle was Rob Davies, a gentle Welshman with a passion for raptors, doing research at the Karoo National Park. Six years previously a fluffy Black Eagle chick was brought to him, the Abel (or less able) of the Cain pair. He trained it to pluck a mouse from his outstretched hand. Now the eagle was fully grown and fully dependent on humans for food. Rob was away for a few days, and Samburu was hungry.

The tale about the chameleon and the lizard is as varied as the number of times it's been told.

The Creator, after Creation, sent a chameleon, Unwabu, to inform men that they would live forever. But on reflection, and being a practical Creator and mindful of over-population, He sent the blue-headed gecko, Intulo, with an amended message, to say that people will die, but not to worry, their spirits will live on forever. However, the

Chameleon

chameleon dallied at the *ubukhwebezane* bush (*Lantana rugosa*), which had ripe fruit on it (according to the story, but since the chameleon doesn't eat fruit, perhaps he was eating the insects that were eating the fruit), thereby being overtaken by the gecko with the new message, which then became gospel.

According to De V. Pienaar, people have a loathing for the chameleon, perhaps rooted in fear, 'for when molested or angered its lungs inflate until the body appears to be near bursting point, the throat is distended, showing the bright orange interstitial skin, the mouth opens wide exposing the red interior. This horrific pose is most impressive and produces an awe-inspiring effect, so much so, that the majority of people regard these creatures with such great fear that no inducement will persuade them to handle specimens.'

Some Zulus believe that the Creator chose the chameleon to deliver the message of Eternity because He knew of its habits, having Himself created it to change colour and thereby deceive. It has a devious eating habit of sitting far from its prey and, at lightning speed, shooting out a long sticky tongue to snatch the victim. It also is abnormal, in that it has five feet! (The tail of the chameleon is said to be a leg coiled around a branch for balance, like a fifth foot.) And just look at those eyes! Where are they looking? You do not know. Forwards, sideways and then backwards. Now one is looking at you and the other one is looking at me. No wonder there is no sympathy for such a thing.

I was not surprised to learn that it takes 6–9 months for the young chameleons to hatch from their eggs, the same time as it takes a human foetus to become fully formed.

~

The fluffy little Martial Eagle chick, on the other hand, takes only 50 days before it breaks open its shell, becoming, within a year, the most magnificent of all the eagles.

Nothing can compare with the thrill of seeing one of these mighty birds surveying its surroundings from the top branches of a dead Leadwood. Their range is now limited to the game reserves and even there it is rarely seen. Direct persecution, pesticides and shrinking habitats are the main causes of their numbers dwindling. Some farmers still believe that a Martial Eagle can kill their sheep and although it is possible for them to tackle a small duiker or a lamb, surely having a pair of these fine birds on the property is a privilege, something to be proud of?

A smaller look-alike of the Martial is the Black-breasted Snake Eagle, and if you have ever wondered why it isn't affected by the venom, Leslie Brown, world-renowned eagle expert, says that 'the rough scales on the snake eagle's legs are supposed to protect them from snake bites but apparently snakes strike mainly at the body and wings of the eagle, to bite only a mouthful of feathers, so that none of the venom enters the eagle's bloodstream'.

~

A crocodile's 'barbarism' can be understood and even excused if one considers its poor physiology. Crocodiles are designed with teeth that are not firm in their sockets, nor can the jaws move from side to side in a chewing motion. So the dead victim has to be left to putrefy under water for a few days for the flesh to become soft and easy to swallow.

The speed with which crocodiles appear out of the water to seize their victim gives rise to the Sotho belief that a crocodile can 'seize' a man's shadow and drag him into its pool.

A Venda tale tells of a big crocodile which arrived in the river. It killed sheep, cattle, herders and traders. The people feared it and did not know how to kill it. One day the chiefs called a meeting to discuss how they might get rid of it.

The jackal came to the meeting and said, 'O Chief, I am small, but wisdom surpasses bravery. Why do you wait for your enemy to grow strong? What do I do? I eat crocodiles while they are still in their eggs. Get rid of your enemy before he is stronger than you.'

Our valley was once known as Mamba Valley and we heard many stories of deadly snakes 'faster than lightning and fatter than your arm'. We were intrigued by the legend of Tony, a tall young man whose hair reportedly went white overnight after he

Martial Eagle bathing

was bitten by a mamba. There have been only a few recorded cases of survival in such cases, so I sought him out to see for myself. True enough, this man had white hair but his father and grandfather had white hair at early ages. The case of the 'mystery of Tony's white hair' was recounted to me by the man himself.

In my early twenties, I was helping on the family farm. On a particularly hot summer's day, we were making hay when I intercepted a snake, disturbed by the tractor. I was suddenly aware of a firm rap on the shin bone. I looked down and saw the snake moving swiftly away. The slender tapering tail, the slate grey colour and its sheer speed said one thing to me, 'Black Mamba'.

I examined my shin and found two fang punctures, with a plasma ooze. Having always had a morbid interest in snakes I knew immediate action was imperative. I hurriedly tied a tourniquet with my handkerchief and asked my labourers if anyone had a pocket knife. In those days it was believed that the wound had to be incised to allow the blood to flow and drain away some of the venom. The knife was so blunt that it failed to break the skin.

I walked to my vehicle (running would have caused the venom to move quickly through the body) and, passing my house, called my servant to accompany me in case I fainted. I drove the 25 kilometres to town at high speed, en route wondering whether to go to a pharmacy or a doctor. Doctors are often out on call or at the hospital, so I elected to go to the pharmacy.

Many thoughts crossed my mind during that journey, death being one of them. Ken Hoggan, a personal friend of mine, was at the counter when I hobbled into his shop. I told him I had been bitten by a mamba or perhaps, with a bit of luck, a Black-necked Cobra. By this time the venom had taken effect and breathing was difficult. I was in a state of shock and the pain at the site of the bite was unbearable. The chemist gave me polyvalent serum intramuscularly. In those days it did not include mamba serum.

His assistant phoned the nearest doctor, who arrived five minutes later. The serum didn't appear to have had any effect, so a separate dose of mamba serum was injected intravenously At this point I was feeling nauseous, sweating profusely and

Black Mamba

in great pain. My entire body had a throbbing 'pins and needles' sensation. Near the site of the bite the calf muscle was in spasm, which continued for hours after the treatment. I lay on the cement floor.

I was confined to bed for two days for observation. The anti-serum causes nausea and some people are allergic to it. Pain pills were given at regular intervals. It was two weeks before I walked without a limp. My saving grace was that I was bitten on the shin bone where there is a meagre blood supply. It was also the end of the snake season and the chances are that the snake had utilised most of its venom.

Ken Hoggan told me later that my sweat outline on the floor took a week to dry out.

The myth of Tony's hair turning white has been supplanted by an even more impressive one. The thought of a sweat outline taking a week to dry out conjures up no less an image than that of the Turin shroud.

~

The Javanese upas tree (*Antiaris toxicaria*) has its roots steeped in mythology. It is thought to be fatal to whatever comes near it. The basis for this belief is the fact that it yields a milky sap toxic enough to be used as arrow poison. We have our own equivalent in the Dead Man's tree (*Synadenium cupulare*), which is a very poisonous tree, credited through superstition with being able to kill at a distance. In former times people would not go near these trees, as a man standing too close would be killed, and the ground around the trees is white with the bones of dead animals. Birds flying directly overhead will fall from the sky.

Medley Wood, a noted collector, wrote, 'After taking the precaution of covering my face, keeping at arm's length from the plant, and carefully washing hands and face as soon as the plants were disposed of, I felt the effects on the eyelids, nostrils and lips for several hours afterwards.'

~

A near-death experience increases Man's need to find a spirituality, a meaningful reason for existence. Most people have a story to tell about their accident, their brush with death, and related to this is usually a bit about how they saw an angel or that their 'lives flashed before their eyes'. Everyone's story will be different but will be as vivid to them as it is personal. And it will change one's life forever.

Ours happened on a Saturday afternoon while the people of the valley were probably watching cricket on television. Lulu Phezulu, our beloved home on the mountain top, moulded now after all these years to suit our tastes and comfort, impregnable and safe, rattled, as yet another storm raged all around us. As we watched in silence, in awe of the force of nature, the storm grew in strength and intensity, the time between the bolt of lightning and the thunder decreasing by the second, then millisecond. We instinctively gravitated to the lounge which has a soft, comfortable atmosphere and a better view through the picture window. I sat in an armchair in the centre of the room, Harry stood behind me, and Max sat down on the window seat. The windowpanes shook and the pelting rain obscured everything. Max got up from his seat close to the window just as a bolt of lightning struck the corner of the room at the very spot where he had just been sitting. A powerful bomb thrown into the room could not have had more impact. The noise was gut-shaking, indescribable. A blinding white shaft of light etched itself somewhere in the brain. When I opened my eyes the air was filled with smoke and debris. The smell of burning plastic and fabric was thick and strong. Concrete bricks from the wall had imploded into the room and shattered, lodging gritty shrapnel into Max's hand, elbows and legs, and in an instant he was across the room, fainting into his father's outstretched arms. He was drained of colour and shaking uncontrollably, but breathing and conscious. We covered him with a blanket, gave him sugar water and phoned the doctor.

Our road after such a huge storm is usually impassable but we had to get Max to the doctor immediately. His hand had been superficially but horribly pitted with blackened grains of wall. His thighs were burnt and bleeding, but most serious was the terrible shock to his system. Harry, who was out of the line of fire, so to speak, was deafened by the blast and three days later still could not hear properly.

The direct strike had been at the base of the outside corner of the room, attracted by the electric cable which lay under the cushions of the window seat. The lightning bolt flashed along the floor, under the carpet, behind the bookcase, up the wall, into the TV, the hi-fi set, amplifier, record player, electric fan, speakers and tape deck. The carpet was shredded and melted, some of it sticking to the ceiling. The wall was scorched sulphur yellow and black, the TV set was blown, the bookcase shattered into matchsticks, and all the other equipment melted and useless. A glass vase lay in shards on a wooden kist, contents pathetically spilled. Black bits of carpet lay scattered all over the room. As the dust and smoke settled we noticed a huge hole in the wall.

Max and Harry returned from the doctor, Max's hands, elbows and legs covered with white bandage. The country doctor had run out of bandage, so covered the wounds with gauze secured by white elastic webbing, which made his thighs and calves look like Kassler rolls. He was in no mood for my analogies. Distress and shock robbed him of his composure and speech. A cup of hot tea and sweet biscuits restored him and he slept.

~

After the Battle at Isandlwana in 1879, when a small garrison of British soldiers was attacked by a horde of 24 000 Zulu warriors, reports of disembowelling and 'mutilation of the dead' were recorded. The British soldiers gazed in horror as the so-called savages cut open the corpses of their victims. But the Zulus were only doing what Catholics in other ways have done for thousands of years – exorcising spirits and avenging ghosts by whom the impis would have been possessed. Besides, the decomposing of unburied bodies under the hot African sun is speeded up and it was essential that the corpses be opened before they began to swell.

~

If you have ever wondered why a hyena circles its prey, the twelfth-century bestiary will tell you that it has a yena in its eye. To you and me that's a stone, which is believed to make a creature able to foresee the future and therefore the possessor of magic skill. With this unusual power, the hyena walks around an animal three times and the animal will not be able to move. (Perhaps the writers of the twelfth-century bestiary had not noticed that there were a couple of lions feeding on the animal round which the hyena was casting his magic spell.)

~

In the rolling lawns of Government House in Bulawayo, Zimbabwe, is a famous tree. King Lobengula, of the Ndebele, gave judgment on matters of life and death under the Indaba Tree, *Pappea capensis*. Pappé, after whom the tree was named, noted that 'the presence of this tree is considered as a criterion of excellent pasture for wool-bearing flocks'. Considering its wide-ranging uses in treatments for anything from loss of hair to venereal diseases, it is surprising that there's anything left of it to boil or infuse, but it is still there and remains what is possibly the earliest example of an 'indicator' plant in Southern Africa.

Umthomboti (*Spirostachys africana*) is common in the flat frost-free Bushveld valleys and its presence is said to indicate acid and sour soil. The wood is to be avoided in the making of fires, burning with a strange sweetish odour causing headaches and nausea while tainting any food cooked over it. While its disadvantages are many, it makes excellent furniture, retaining its distinctive smell for many years. Sitting in a shady grove of *umthomboti* trees, one may notice a liveliness in the fallen seeds. They are often infested with the larvae of a small grey moth, which, by spasmodic straightening of the body, causes the seed to spring several centimetres into the air.

~

Man's shortcomings can be treated with Mother Nature's bountiful balms.

Axel-Ivar Berglund informs us that 'Talkativeness is treated with parts of a sheep, the animal being a symbol of quietness; a man with particularly short legs was once treated with bones obtained from a stork.'

J.H. Yates maintains that 'even as late as the eighteenth century, the Daddy-long-legs spider was used as a cure for malaria, folded up and put in a raisin'.

Leprosy was claimed to have been effectively checked by administering medicines containing flesh from pythons. Pythons symbolise togetherness, 'not allowing flesh to fall off the body'. It was also used for people whose thoughts tended to stray.

Fear and anxiety are treated with flesh from animals that are said to have no fear, and parts of the Common Mole were used to treat mental disorders.

Men who are unable to obtain erection are given infusions of *inthwalabombo* (*Rubia cordifolia*), a species of climbing plant said to be soft and bendable without breaking off.

*Pill
beetles*

'A man refused by girls because he is considered ugly becomes handsome in their eyes if he is treated with a decoction prepared by boiling *ibhuma* (the common bulrush) in milk, that of a goat. Bulrushes are said to have no flowers (Zulus who recognise the flower say that it is ugly). The ugliness of the growth and the animal produce handsomeness in the male.'

If dogs appear to sleep too much, medicine is prepared from *imfinyezi* (*isipungu mangathi*) or Pill Beetle (a beetle that curls up when touched), and given to the animal to prevent it from being like the beetle.

If eating ground-up beetles helps dogs to regulate their sleeping disorders, Nietzsche has another remedy for us. 'Avoid all who sleep badly and stay awake at night. Sleeping is no mean art, for its sake one must stay awake all day. Ten times a day you must overcome yourself: that makes you good and tired and is opium for the soul. Ten times you must reconcile yourself again with yourself; for overcoming is bitterness and the unreconciled sleep badly. Ten truths a day you must find, else you will still be seeking truth by night, and your soul will remain hungry. Ten times a day you must laugh and be cheerful; else you will be disturbed at night by your stomach, this father of gloom.'

～

The Lowveld, like most small communities, has its eccentric characters. Roland was a gentle man, kind and affable. Except when it came to Red-winged Starlings. Their incessant knocking of their beaks against the windowpane drove Roland mad. He had tried everything. In desperation he resorted to murder – cold, cruel, calculated decapitation. He plotted for weeks and then devised his plan. He consumed vast quantities of wine for the lead which secures the cork, and melted it down in a large pot on the kitchen stove to form a heavy blade with a loop at the top. Through the loop he tied a piece of nylon cord which he threaded through other loops and pulleys leading from above the lounge window, through the fanlight, across the ceiling and down the opposite wall, just to the right of Roland's favourite chair. When a male starling thought he saw another male starling in the reflection in the glass window, he would tap-tap-tap with his beak. But not anymore. Without leaving his favourite chair or even looking up from his book, Roland could activate the deadly guillotine with the flick of his wrist, and another Red-winged Starling would bite the dust, his head neatly severed at

*A pink gladiolus
with a virtue*

the neck. It took a day or two before another Red-winged Starling would spot a supposed rival in Roland's window and repeat the tap-tap-tap dance. But not for long. Roland would be ready.

~

Insanity, believed to be caused by excessive brooding of the shades, is treated with medicines prepared of feathers and skin from a vulture, because they fly very high up in the sky, far from the earth, where the shades are.

The pink gladiolus, *Gladiolus ludwigii*, now *G. sericeo-villosus*, has a virtue in its root which helps to increase the productiveness of the crops if the planter places it amongst the seed while she is doing the sowing. If the skin of the nut-like roots is intact and hard, then it is healthy and alive and the radicle can burst out and grow. It is the same with the seeds of the maize. Rot and pests cause the seeds to be soft or damaged. Destruction comes from outside.

While on my travels in KwaZulu-Natal I was introduced to a local man named Simon who had toothache. The next day, sans dentist, he was smiling. He had sniffed of the concurbit root, *Coccinia rehmannii*. He explained how he had taken the root of the plant, placed it in a metal box through which he had punched some holes, lit a candle underneath, and allowed the fumes to float into his open mouth for an hour or two, and *voila*, pain gone!

Bald men are believed to be infertile and their predicament is treated with medicines from gardens with a profuse growth.

I grew up roughing it, camping out – and ignorance was bliss. Lying cocooned in a sleeping bag on the day-warmed desert sand under the stars was my idea of heaven. Only when I travelled with arachnophiles Astri and Jean-Marie Leroy, who were equipped with a portable ultraviolet light which illuminates scorpions in the dark, did I realise my past foolishness. Having come out of their burrows to forage at night, the scorpions large and small glowed a luminous lime green. They scurried around underfoot in their hundreds making me wish I could fly or at least levitate, and convinced me that one should never sleep on the ground.

To be stung by a scorpion is like 'flaming bullets twisting inside you' and can reduce a macho ranger to tears. There are two types of scorpions in southern Africa: the more

The scorpion is as black as soot,
he dearly loves to bite;
He is a most unpleasant brute
To find in bed, at night.
— HILLAIRE BELLOC

dangerous one has small pincers and a big sting pouch at the tip of a thick tail.

Parabuthus villosus is a large scorpion found in the Namib Desert and is able to squirt its venom into your eyes from quite a distance.

Nicotine juice from a pipe relieves pain and swelling in a scorpion sting, so does ammonia, petrol or paraffin. A six-year-old child, stung in the finger, whose parents plunged the finger into a fresh hen's egg and made the child keep it there for thirty minutes, suffered no pain or ill effects, but the egg is reported to have turned blue.

The scorpion, for all its sins, is a remarkable creation, a model conserver of energy and resources, able to go without food for up to a year and to withstand extreme heat and cold, is found on the dunes of the deserts where temperatures soar to the mid-40°C and in the icy Himalayas at 14 000 feet.

A very common fern on the koppies around Lulu Phezulu is *Pellea calomelanos*, growing at the base of rocks, managing to survive in tiny pockets of soil. An extract of the rhizome may be applied to boils or administered in milk to a frightened child.

Our children trained themselves not to be frightened and to keep quiet about their boils. Mother was experimenting with herbal remedies and was on the look-out for ailments with which to experiment.

When we watched a lizard lose its tail to the cat and grow a new one, the males in my family went missing for three days.

Dr Lewis Thomas pondered the intricacies of dying in his book *The Medusa and the Snail*. 'The dying of a field mouse, at the jaws of an amiable household cat, is a spectacle I have beheld many times. It used to make me wince. Early in life I gave up throwing sticks at the cat to make him drop the mouse, because the dropped mouse regularly went ahead and died anyway, but I always shouted unaffections at the cat to let him know the sort of animal he had become. *Nature*, I thought, was an abomination.'

To seek a balance or a contrast from the green lush tropical vegetation of our valley, and to discover new root remedies, we travelled frequently to arid brown places. One such visit was north, to a certain part of Venda, to pay homage to a tree. No ordinary tree, though. This is one of the biggest Baobabs (*Adansonia digitata*) in existence. One falls silent in the company of a tree whose girth measures no less than forty-three metres.

Looking around I was pleased to note that there are some young trees in the vicin-

He that plants trees loves others besides himself.
— THOMAS FULLER

ity, because until recently there was a belief amongst the locals that there was no such thing as a young Baobab. Not surprising since the bark of the young plants is soft and fibrous and used as ropes in the building of their houses. Now that most homes are built with bricks the young Baobabs may grow to maturity.

The Baobab, one of Africa's most venerated trees, generates a wealth of legend and superstition.

According to some tribes the seeds and plants were distributed by the gods to the animals of the world to cultivate. Last of all the plants was the Baobab, which was issued to the hyena, who, being stupid, planted it upside down.

Furthermore, anyone rash enough to pluck a flower from a Baobab will be devoured by a lion, for the blooms are believed to be inhabited by spirits. It is also said that a sip of water in which the seeds have been soaked will act as protection against attack by a crocodile and that a man who drinks an infusion of the bark will become mighty and strong.

David Livingstone, the explorer, during one of his most difficult treks, was suffering from malaria and was kept alive by imbibing vast quantities of this drink. Perhaps it was not unlike my gingerbeer.

According to Piet van Wyk there are other trees that are bigger than the one we visited but we were quite happy with our tree. Except for one thing. The tree has recently been made accessible to the public and consequently has 'RAYMOND LOVES DENISE' and 'PIET 1989' freshly etched into its soft flesh. I wept with rage for the rape of its pristine 5000-year-old skin.

MAN, *I* think, is the abomination.

The Baobab has been a sacred tree for generations of sangomas, inyangas and herbalists, who come to it to renew their magical powers. In the valleys nearby are flaked tools left by inhabitants of the Later Stone Age who probably could once have put their arms around its sapling stomach.

The Leadwood (*hardekool* or *Combretum imberbe*), to most people, is simply choice braai-wood, but the Hereros of Namibia consider it to be the Ancestral Tree from which came humans, their stock and wild animals. It is truly a magnificent symbol of longevity, so much so, that David Livingstone's devoted porters thought that its pro-

tective durability would be a fitting place under which to bury his heart. The rest of him was embalmed, covered with tar and carried over a thousand kilometres to Dar es Salaam, from where a ship took him to his final resting place in Westminster Abbey.

~

There are many euphemisms for the word 'dying', but none prove so confusing as the word 'late'.

Sue managed a local garden shop and one of her faithful employees, although a good worker, was never on time. One day he took ill and during the next few weeks Sue took him regularly for treatment to hospital. As usual she called for him at the arranged time but was told, 'I'm sorry, Mr Ndlovu is late.'

'Yes, I know,' said Sue, 'he's always late.'

'No, you don't understand,' insisted the nurse. 'He's late.'

Sue's embarrassment was evident as soon as she realised that her faithful worker was now deceased. The late Mr Ndlovu.

~

The last word in scary creatures, with its skull-like markings on the thorax, must surely be the Death's Head Hawkmoth, *Acherontia atropos*. It feeds not only on the dagga plant, but on the bugweed, an invasive weed belonging to the highly poisonous Deadly Nightshade family (*Atropa*). When it raids beehives it emits an awesome series of squeaks and hisses which, it is said, sound like the pre-swarming piping of the queen bee. Also, when handled, these fearsome moths issue bloodcurdling hisses, which cause me to recall the legend of Atropos. She was depicted with a veiled face and a pair of scissors to cut the thread of life.

Talking of dying, our *Aloe bainesii*, which we had grown from a cutting, died on the same day as Liberace. It had been a fine specimen, tall and sturdy. On that fateful day, I nonchalantly stretched out my arm and leaned against it and my hand sank wrist-deep into the termite-chewed fibre. What degree of drought, disease or neglect is needed to cause a plant to become moribund, to the point of no revival? To ascertain the precise moment of its demise is apparently not possible. It has no heart, only a lettuce has a heart. Is wilt merely malaise?

~

The last moments of George's life were grotesque. Picture a gentleman, the epitome of style, taste and intellect, an Oxford scholar, fluent in eleven languages, living in luxurious splendour surrounded by the plantations that made him the wealthiest man in the valley. Intolerant of fools ('Imbeciles!'), derogatory about his ex-wife ('Couldn't boil an egg!'), he lavished all his energies on fine food, the finest wine, music and his books – a huge library consisting of the best collection of flora and fauna Africana in the country. His funeral was a wake, a splendid affair under the *Schizolobium*s, now fifty metres tall, which he had planted fifty years before. Damask linen cloths covered tables that groaned with mounds of crayfish in silver tureens, strawberries and crème fraîche, melba toasts and Earl Grey tea.

For a few coins on the bedside table and a pair of trousers, his last gasp was taken beneath the barbaric tightening of his own pyjama cord around his neck. A petty thief had come in through a skylight and George, having dined well that evening, was in a deep sleep. But when woken and startled he was like a raging bull, judging by the amount of damage found by the police in the bedroom. Had the thief known the value of the Ming vases, the Bokharas and first editions, he might have done better to have tackled a different room and let George sleep in peace and at least wake up in the morning.

~

I never had the honour of meeting her, but Emily Greathead became a legend in our valley. She bypassed laws, befriended rich and poor alike, and ruled over her estate with a rod of iron and a sensitive plough. She ran one of the best farms in the area. Once, when she did not want the new provincial road to go through her orchard, she knew what strings to pull, and from then on cars and trucks had to execute a seemingly inexplicable, unexpected and dangerous hairpin bend. Little did she know that during the next fifty years or so, fifty people would lose their lives on that corner. On reaching the age of 105 she was visited by a young journalist in awe of her reputation. After his interview he said, 'Mrs Greathead, it has been a privilege, I do hope I will be able to interview you on your next birthday.'

Her answer was to the point. 'Why, young man, are you not well?'

~

One advantage of living in a small community for a long time is that bonds are

established between neighbours, parents of school-going children, and then the children themselves. Births, graduations and marriages, all the rites of passage are observed, giving a sense of belonging. When a much-loved member of the community dies, a wave of collective grief and consciousness joins everyone in a shared experience.

When Graeme died suddenly it was difficult to accept. He was a hero, a good-looking, blue-eyed, soft-spoken Canadian pilot, a scientist of the clouds. He ran a company which researched the seeding of clouds with chemicals, a hail suppression scheme designed to protect the tobacco crop from being damaged by hailstones. Graeme would fly his jet into the heart of a cumulus storm cloud in a courageous attempt to entice the might of Mother Nature to spread her bounty over a wider farming area in the form of gentle rain. The scheme met with opposition from some farmers who did not care how the rain fell as long as it fell, but others praised his work, inviting him to deliver lectures throughout the world. We'd look up at the sky on a hot summer's day to watch the storm clouds gather, and there, like a little white bird, was Graeme, in his element, weaving magic into his beloved clouds. But when the Big C claimed his mortal frame, his last wish was to be returned to the skies.

We were all gathered together, as the helicopter carrying his ashes circled overhead. One minute's silence was observed as the clouds swirled, the helicopter hung suspended, and Graeme's ashes were cast to the wind. A freak condensation formed them into a celestial cloud which caught the light and then dispersed, wafting gently into the ether.

Many die too late, and a few die too early.

To end on a hopeful note, there is a plant called the Resurrection plant, *Myrothamnus flabellifolius,* which grows in shallow pockets of soil on dry and exposed granite slopes. In times of drought the rusty-red leaves are closely packed and folded together along the short incurved branches of this bushy little shrub, presenting an apparently dead condition, but they become fully expanded and a rich healthy green after a good shower or if soaked in water.

Nature is most forgiving.

chapter nine

of
Mice and Men

And now for the future. What does it hold? What has Nature planned for us? We are inextricably tied to the umbilical cord of Mother Earth and although the destiny of a handful of scientists might be to tramp in the dust of distant planets, the rest of us would do well to study the life history of the Multimammate Mouse (*Praomys natalensis*). The parallel with humans is unsettling.

The Multimammate Mouse is common and widespread, small and grey, is attracted to cities and breeds throughout the year. The young are born helpless and hairless, covered by a pink, translucent skin.

Could be you and me.

They urinate and defecate in designated toilet areas and are peaceful and tolerant of other rodents. They twitter when content. Yet they are wary animals and are easily alarmed. The alarm or defence note is a harsh screech.

Could be you and me.

They can start breeding at an early age, giving birth at regular intervals, which means that their numbers increase markedly to unprecedented levels in a short space of time. When this occurs, the phenomenon is described by mammologists as a population explosion.

Oh really?

Between 1960 and 1965, and then again in 1992, the whole of southern Africa suffered a serious drought. Then the heavy rains came, which resulted in lush growth over large parts of the country. One study area was around Lake Ngami in Botswana where populations of mice and gerbils were reaching extraordinarily high levels. They swarmed everywhere. The increase continued for two years, after which time their numbers were so vast that they began to self-destruct.

'Specimens that were collected were diseased – showing swollen lumps on the feet, on the reproductive tract and scrotal sacs, with uteri often grossly deformed. Cannibalism was rife.'

Could be you and me.

~

Our sleepy valley awoke one morning to the news that a crazed killer was on the loose in the forests. We had always felt immune to the stresses of city life but it seems that the human condition is the same wherever one chooses to live.

The story goes that a senior employee of a large company had repeatedly told his supervisor that the fleet of trucks carrying heavy equipment was being inadequately maintained and that the drivers were insufficiently trained. He was a perfectionist, some would say obsessional, but in the end he became so persistent in his accusations that he was dismissed from the company. His frustrations were increased by the fact that he had recently separated from his wife and, with his sacking, his financial troubles would now worsen. He was already at breaking point, so when the car in which he and his soon-to-be-ex-wife were driving was hit by one of the errant trucks he snapped. He attacked the driver, stormed into the nearby supervisor's office, pulled out a pistol and shot him, and all the rest of the people in the office, dead. His rage spent and now a wanted man, he came to his senses, took his soon-to-be-ex-wife to hospital and made for the hills.

As in all small communities, everyone soon passed judgment, claimed to have known him for years, claimed to have seen him in a forest, even claimed the reward, and all related their own version of what could have happened. Everyone became instant experts in the law, in psychology. For eight days he became the nation's most wanted man, a scarlet pimpernel. People were baying for blood, the hounds were out to get him. Mostly the news hounds in this case. The simple fact of the matter was that stress had surfaced and erupted in a violent manner, leaving a trail of widows, orphans and tragedy in its wake.

It could easily have happened to you or me.

To pay for his legal costs all his possessions were sold and the community rallied to help the families pick up the pieces. He got fourteen years and Doreen got his goldfish.

Being human is to defy nature. We strive to curb natural diseases, which are sent to manage the population. We prolong the agony of a terminally ill patient, we persevere with growing exotic plants in desert areas, we get upset when our rivers dry up, yet still plant more timber and sugar cane. We eat foods that rot our teeth and tax our livers. As humans responsible for our own lives we can control our destinies and fulfil our

ambitions. We should show compassion when it's due whilst believing in the survival of the fittest.

In our dog-eat-dog world (I've never known the origin of that expression but it sounds disgustingly apt for our society), little cognisance is taken of the fact that we are being desensitised.

From my mountaintop eyrie I acknowledge that we were indeed privileged humans to have lived in a wilderness area but feel guilty at our impact on this little piece of Africa, which is irreversible. A newly cleared site for a developer is like a gash in a little girl's cheek. The wilderness is fragile, virgin. People should be barred from pristine wild areas. Trails, hikes, night drives are supposed to give us a wilderness experience but we take along our pollutants, our debris: leave behind a trail of toilet paper and learn nothing. Let the People throng to man-made theme parks. Let Nature be. Long, long ago we as humans lost our respect for Nature, lost our ability to be in touch with Her song.

Each morning I walked from the house down the steep hillside to the stream with our small dog Spike. On a cool drizzly Tuesday, as we scrambled our way back up the path, Spike suddenly yelped, exploded out of the grass and almost leapt into my arms with fright. A Bushpig stood squarely before us. Fortunately he only grunted and moved off, allowing us to pass. Bushpigs are dangerous, particularly if startled or cornered. If they are with young they are likely to react with a vicious swipe of their sharp tusks.

So the next morning, since all God's children know that Bushpigs live in valleys, we walked up the hill, to the plateau on *top* of the mountain. No bushpigs *there*. When we got to the top, Spike's hackles rose as his sharp ears picked up a rustling in the dense undergrowth. I stopped to listen and, sure enough, more than one was coming towards us this time. Sounded more like ten. Spike made off in the opposite direction and I climbed a big sturdy tree and sat and waited. I figured that if they hadn't picked up our scent they would pass directly below the branch on which I was sitting. I held my breath and my heart thumped as the armada approached, snuffling and snorting, their feet crushing the leaves and twigs. I strained to see them but could only detect a rustling of the tall grass and a movement in the lower branches. Then my cell phone rang. I nearly fell out of the tree. Of course they moved off, and Spike and I made our way home for breakfast.

When our children were small and in need of consolation or sympathy we would to send them down to the Thinking Tree. The chosen magic tree was a Kiaat (*Pterocarpus angolensis*), just far enough away for them to have forgotten their problem by the time they got there. Through the years it became our symbol of Energy, Strength and Life, and whenever we passed it, either on foot or in the car, we had to reach out and touch it. We fully believed that it gave us the power to conquer the world, solve our problems and heal our wounds. Last year the Lowveld experienced one of the worst droughts in history. Yes, you guessed it. The magic Kiaat died. Having known all along that I was foolish to have placed so much faith in a helpless tree, it nevertheless preyed on my mind.

The power of symbolism, myth and magic holds us in thrall, even a sceptic like me.

Twenty-five years ago Robert Ardrey came for lunch. He got out of the car, wiped his brow (the humidity was unusually high that day), and walked to the very spot where Harry had stood on that first day many years ago. With an expansive gesture he embraced the sky, the mountains, the world.

'Just look at that Vlaminck sky!'

The clouds were about to do what they had done many times before, turn purple and explode.

Then he broke bread with us, homemade wholewheat bread, and we sipped cool wine. The heavens opened up and we sat in awe of yet another magnificent African storm.

In his speech in 1977 at the World Wilderness Congress, and long before the Greenhouse Effect, Aids and the Hole in the Ozone Layer had become part of daily conversation, Robert Ardrey predicted that by the turn of the century, instead of the population of the earth doubling, it would be halved.

He was not prepared to take a guess as to whether it would be a new Ice Age or a mutated virus which would be the end of most of us, but it appears that he could have put his money on both.

As for us, we opted to choose another magic tree to replace the dead one, and to continue to believe that it will protect us from whatever Mother Nature has in store.

Such is the Spirit of Man.

And Woman.

B UT YOU WHO ARE WISE *must know that different Nations have different Conceptions of things and you will therefore not take it amiss, if our Ideas of this kind of Education happen not to be the same as yours. We have had some experience of it. Several of our young People were formerly brought up at the Colleges of the Northern Provinces: they were instructed in all your Sciences: but, when they came back to us, they were bad Runners, ignorant of every means of living in the woods, neither fit for Hunters, Warriors, nor Counsellors, They were totally good for nothing. We are, however, not the less oblig'd by your kind Offer, tho' we decline accepting it; and, to show our grateful Sense of it, if the Gentlemen of Virginia will send us a Dozen of their Sons, we will take Care of their Education, instruct them in all we know, and make Men of them.*

— RESPONSE OF THE INDIANS OF THE SIX NATIONS TO A SUGGESTION THAT THEY SEND BOYS TO AN AMERICAN COLLEGE, PENNSYLVANIA, 1744

ACKNOWLEDGEMENTS

No book of this nature is possible without the support of sponsors. Steve Bales of First National Bank, a stalwart, a friend, passionate about nature and art, generously kick-started the project.

I thank Barbara Jeppe, my beloved mother, for thousands of snippets of information from her unfathomable store of knowledge about every aspect of the bush, and the very happy field trips we shared together:

Dr Carl Jeppe, my father, for his unbridled encouragement in everything I have ever done and his awakening in me, at a very early age, a hunger to explore and the capacity for astonishment when I find it:

Max, my first-born, for his genuine belief that I should persevere with this personal indulgence, his helpful comments and supernatural patience with my ignorance of the computer:

Walter, my younger son, who throughout his childhood supplied me with beetles and snakes, birds and plants, rocks and butterflies, and then, when he grew up, encouraged me and helped me immeasurably:

Harry, my husband, who passed a critical eye over everything I did, and then simply said 'yes' to it.

I am deeply grateful to Warwick Tarboton for the use of some of his photographs and for checking my bird facts, to Elisabeth Lickindorf for her meticulous combing of the manuscript for grammatical errors, to Dr Graham Baker for ensuring that my scientific facts were reasonably accurate.

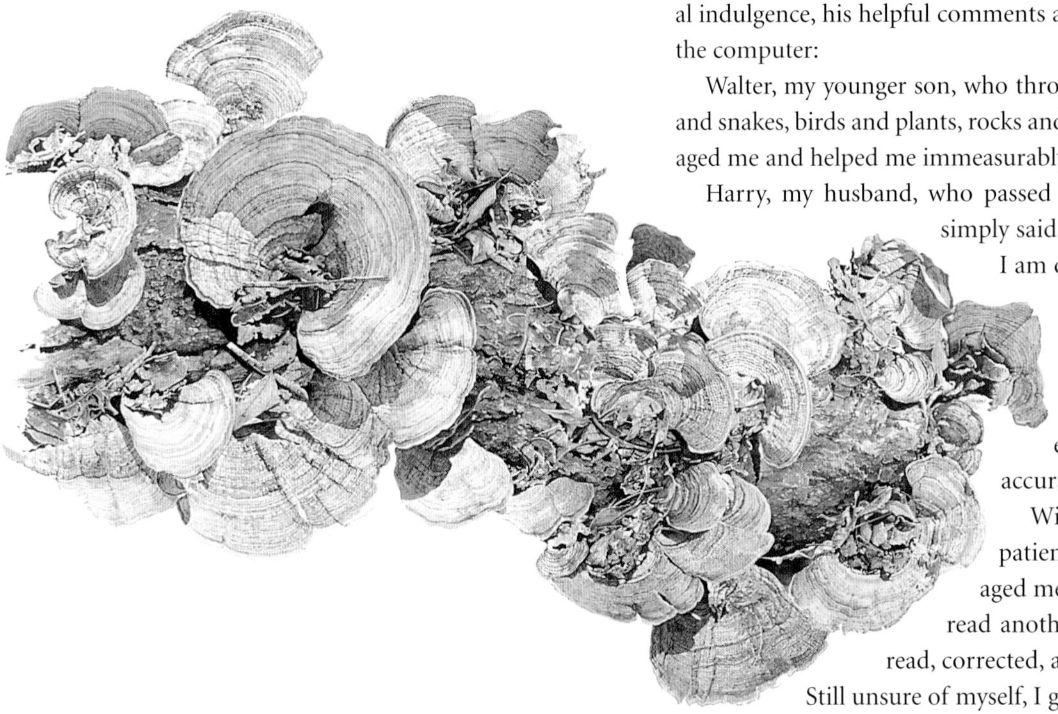

Wilf Nussey checked my original manuscript, patiently introduced me to the computer and encouraged me to proceed, pushing me all the way. Kevin Gill read another attempt and kept me on course. Tony Hall read, corrected, advised and encouraged me in yet another draft. Still unsure of myself, I gave it to my brother David Jeppe, whose suggestions were invaluable. Dr Günter Schlosser lovingly supported me when my spirits flagged. I thank John and Astri Leroy for their infectious enthusiasm and for the times we spent in special places, and Scott Ronaldson for exquisite days at Pafuri.

I am indebted to my cousin Marguerite Poland, who was with me in spirit all the way.

A book of this nature is not possible without input from many sources, so I gleaned warps and wefts from all over the country and wove a colourful fabric, presenting it as if it were my own. I have plagiarised Palmer and Palgrave, robbed Roberts, stolen from the Stuarts, climbed into Messrs Branch and Burrows, borrowed from Bannister, Braack and Boycott, walked with Clive, loaned from Ledger, devoured Codd, Wood and Cotton, dived into Pooley, used my Brain, got Goode and Giddy, and generally had fun.

Many people, consciously or otherwise, have contributed in one way or another and to them, one and all, I am deeply grateful. From the twenty or so years it has taken me to get this far, whilst doing other things in between (for I never expected to get this far), many names spring to mind, for having either shared a piece of interesting information, or lent a photograph, given advice, corrected a mistake, supplied materials, or generously given of their time.

In alphabetical order: Lisa Bryson, Shane Burns, Eleanor Mary Cadell, Archie Clarke, Bryce Courtenay, Peter and Ute Fellenberg, Tessa Fleischer, Naomi Fourie, Anne Graupner, Tony Haig, Dorothy Hall, Eddie Harris, Gavin Heimann, Kotie Heroldt, Paul and Marc Leroy, Marie MaCrae, Cally Mail, Neil McCormick, Doug McMurtry, Clare Nevin, Jo Onderstal, Doug Starling, Vic Swarts, Phillip Tetley, Peter van der Merwe, Simon Zuma.

I also want to thank the many people who own the paintings reproduced in this book. I could not acknowledge you all personally but sincerely appreciate your silent support. You have helped make this book. And Girlie Ngomane, without whose help this book could not have been written.

BIBLIOGRAPHY

Allan, David. *Quagga*, No. 24, 1988.

Andersson, Charles John. *Lake Ngami*, C. Struik, Cape Town, reprint 1967.

Arnold, G. A *Monograph of the Formicidae of South Africa*, Annals of the South African Museum, 14.

Berglund, Axel-Ivar. *Zulu Thought Patterns and Symbolism*. C. Hurst, London, 1976.

Brain, Prof C.K. *The Hunters or the Hunted? An Introduction to African Cave Taphonomy*, The University of Chicago Press, Chicago, 1981.

Brown, Leslie. *Birds of Prey: Their Biology and Ecology*, Hamlyn, London 1976.

Burton, Maurice. *The Sixth Sense of Animals*, J.M. Dent, London, 1973.

Catton, Chris and Gray, James. *Sex in Nature*, Croom Helm, London, 1985.

Clarke, James. *The Sunday Star Review*, 14 June 1987.

Comrie-Greig, John. *African Wildlife*, Vol. 45, No. 4, and Vol. 39, No. 5.

Cooke, M.C. *Freaks and Marvels of Plant Life*, London.

Cooper, Sue and Van Hoven, Wouter. *Fauna and Flora*, 1987.

Craig, Adrian. *Birding in South Africa*, Dec. 1989.

De Graaff, G. *The Rodents of Southern Africa*, Butterworths, Durban, 1981.

De Graaff, G. 'Man and Molluscs Hosts to Schistosoma', *Custos*, April 1985.

De Villiers, Atherton and Picker, Mike. *African Wildlife*, Vol. 43, No. 3.

Dickinson, Colin and Lucas, John. *The Encyclopaedia of Mushrooms*, Orbis Publishing, London, 1979.

Drosscher, Vitus B. *They Love and Kill: Sex, Sympathy and Aggression in Courtship and Mating*, E.P. Dutton, New York.

Drosscher, Vitus B. *The Magic of the Senses*, W.H. Allen, London, 1969.

Eibl-Eibersfeldt, Irenaus. *Ethology: The Biology of Behaviour*, Holt, Rinehart and Winston, New York, 1970.

Emboden, William A. *Bizarre Plants*, Cassell & Collier Macmillan Publishers, London, 1974.

Falk, Greta. *African World*, Dec. 1954.

Fourie, P.B. *Fauna and Flora*, No. 43, 1986.

Froman, Robert. *Spiders and Other Outcasts*, G. Bell and Sons, London, 1965.

Fox, Francis and Young, Marion Norwood. *Food from the Veld*, Delta Books, Johannesburg, 1982.

Funk and Wagnall's Standard Dictionary of Folklore, Mythology and Legend, 1949.

Giddy, Cynthia. *Cycads of South Africa*, Purnell, Cape Town, 1974.

Godfrey, Rev. Robert. *Bird Lore of the Eastern Cape Province*, Witwatersrand University Press, Johannesburg, 1941.

Gordon, Lesley. *Green Magic*, Webb and Bower, Exeter, 1977.

Green, Lawrence G. *A Taste of South-Easter*, Timmins, Cape Town, 1971.

Green, Lawrence G. *In the Land of Afternoon*, Timmins, Cape Town, 1949.

Guy, R.D. *African Wildlife*, Vol. 25.

Haw, Richard C. 'Wildlife and African Folklore', *Custos* Vol. 20, No. 9, December 1991.

Henning, Stephen F. and Graham A. *South African Red Data Book – Butterflies*, Pretoria 1989.

Highfield, Roger. *The Weekly Telegraph*, Issue No. 231.

Isemonger, R.M. *Snakes of Africa*, Books of Africa, Cape Town, 1968.

Jaff, Fay. *Looking at Nature in South Africa*, Timmins, Cape Town, 1966.

Johnston, Peter. *The Guardian*, reprinted in the *Weekly Mail*, December 1 to December 7, 1989.

Karmali, J. *Birds of Africa*, Viking Press, New York, 1980.

Knappert, Jan. *The Aquarian Guide to African Mythology*, Aquarian Press, part of the Thorsons Publishing Group, London, 1990.

Lawrence, R.F.A. *A Conspectus of South African Spiders*, Department of Agricultural Technical Services, Natal Museum, Pietermaritzburg, November 1964.

Levin, H., Branch, M., Rappoport, S., and Mitchell, D. *A Field Guide to the Mushrooms of South Africa*, C. Struik, Cape Town, 1985.

Lorus, J. and Milne, Margery. *Balance of Nature*, Alfred A. Knopf, New York, 1972.

Lucas, Annabelle and Hancock, Florence D. *Ferns of the Witwatersrand*, Witwatersrand University Press, Johannesburg, 1973.

Macdonald, Ian. *Birding in South Africa*, Vol. 44, No. 1, March 1992.

Maclean, Gordon. *Roberts Birds of Southern Africa*, Published by the Trustees of the John Voelcker Bird Book Fund, Cape Town, first published 1940.

Marais, Eugene. *The Soul of the White Ant*, Penguin, Harmondsworth, reprint 1973.

Mills, M.G.L. *Kalahari Hyaenas: The Comparative Behavioural Ecology of Two Species*, Unwin Hyman, London, 1990.

Möller, P. Translated by Ione and Jalmar Rudner. *Journey through Angola, Ovamboland and Damaraland, 1895–1896*, C. Struik, Cape Town, 1974. Original Swedish edition 1899.

Mouton, Shona. *African Wildlife*, Vol. 42, No. 6.

Nature Thoughts, A Selection. Edited by Louise Bachelder, Peter Pauper Press, Mount Vernon, New York, 1965.

Newman, Ken. *Birdlife in Southern Africa*, Purnell, Johannesburg, 1971.

New Scientist, 15 May 1986, 28 November 1985, 3 April 1986, 24 April 1986

Nuttall, R.J. *Ostrich*, Vol. 63, No. 2 and 3, September 1992.

Oldroyd, Harold. *Elements of Entomology*, Weidenfeld and Nicolson, London, 1968.

Opie, Iona and Tatem, Moira. *A Dictionary of Superstitions*, Oxford University Press, Oxford, 1989.

The Oxford Companion to Animal Behaviour. Edited by David McFarland, Oxford University Press, Oxford, 1987.

Palgrave, Keith Coates. *Trees of Southern Africa*, C. Struik, Cape Town, 1977.

Parrinder, Geoffrey. *African Mythology*, Hamlyn, Middlesex, 1967.

Peattie, Donald Culross. The Web of Life, *American Horticulturist*, October 1991.

Phillips, Roger. *Mushrooms and Other Fungi of Great Britain and Europe*, Ward Lock, London, 1981.

Pienaar, U de V. *The Reptile Fauna of the Kruger National Park*, National Parks Board of South Africa, Pretoria, 1978.

Pienaar, U. de V., Passmore, N.I. and Carruthers, V.C. *The Frogs of the Kruger National Park*, National Parks Board of South Africa, Pretoria, 1976.

Pinhey, E.C.G. *Moths of Southern Africa*, Tafelberg, Cape Town, 1975.

Pirow, Oswald. *Shangani*, Dagbreek, Johannesburg, 1953.

Pooley, Elsa. *The Complete Field Guide to Trees of Natal, Zululand and Transkei*, Natal Flora Publications Trust, 1993.

Purnell's Encyclopaedia of Animal Life, Vol. 1, No. 6.

Rasa, Anne. *Mongoose Watch*, John Murray, London, 1985.

Sagan, Carl. *The Dragons of Eden*, Hodder and Stoughton, London, 1977.

Samuelson, D.C. *Long, Long Ago*, Knox Printing and Publishing Company, Durban, 1929.

Samuelson, L.H. *Zululand, Its Traditions, Legends, Customs and Folk-lore*, Griggs, Durban, 1974.

Savory, Phyllis. *Custos*, Vol. 16, No. 1.

Scholtz, Clarke and Holm, Erik. *Insects of Southern Africa*, Butterworths, Durban, 1985.

Shkolnick, Amiram. *Nature*, 283, 373, reprinted in *South African Science Journal*, Vol. 76, May 1980.

Shuker, Karl. *Extraordinary Animals Worldwide*, Robert Hale, London.

Simons, Paul. *The Action Plant: Movement and Nervous Behaviour in Plants*, Blackwell, Oxford, 1992.

Skaife, S.H. *African Insect Life*, Struik Publishers, Cape Town, revised edition 1979.

Smith, C.A. *Common Names of South African Plants*, Department of Agricultural Technical Services, Government Printer, Pretoria, 1966.

Smithers, R.H.N. *The Mammals of the Southern African Subregion*, University of Pretoria, Pretoria, 1983.

Steyn, Peter. *Getaway Magazine*, October 1993.

Stuart, Chris and Tilde, *African Wildlife*, Vol. 43, No.1, 1989.

Swanepoel, D.A. *Butterflies of South Africa: Where, When and How They Fly*, Maskew Miller, Cape Town, 1953.

Sweeney, James Johnson and Radin, Paul. *African Folk Tales and Sculpture*, Bollingen Series, Princeton University Press, New Haven, 1952 and 1964.

Tarboton, Dr Warwick. *Fauna and Flora*, No. 45, 1987.

Tedder, Vivian. *The People of a Thousand Hills*, C. Struik, Cape Town, 1968.

Tompkins, Peter and Bird, Christopher. *The Secret Life of Plants*, London, Allen Lane, revised edition 1974.

Thomas, Lewis. *The Medusa and the Snail*, London, Allen Lane, 1979.

Thomas, Lewis. *The Lives of a Cell*, Viking Press, New York, 1974.

Tredgold, Sir Robert. *Xhosa: Tales of Life from the African Veld*, Allen and Unwin, London, 1973.

Van Wyk, Piet. *Trees of the Kruger National Park*, Purnell, Johannesburg, 1972.

Wager, Vincent A. *Frogs of Southern Africa*, Delta Books, Johannesburg, 1986.

Watson, Chris and Richard. *Custos*, Vol. 14, No. 8, November 1985.

Werner, Alice. *Myths and Legends of the Bantu*, George G. Harrap, London, 1933.

Wood, Gerald L. *The Guinness Book of Animal Facts and Feats*, Guinness, Middlesex, 1972.

Wrogemann, Nan. *Cheetah under the Sun*, McGraw-Hill, Johannesburg, 1975.

Yates, J.H. *Spiders of Southern Africa*, Books of Africa, Cape Town, 1968.

Zeitlmayr, Linus. *Wild Mushrooms*, Frederick Muller, London, 1955.

THE AUTHOR

LEIGH VOIGT was born to a botanical artist mother and a psychiatrist father with the result that she grew up in nature reserves and mental homes. Her training was at the Johannesburg School of Art;, thereafter she spent seven years in advertising studios. Since then she has had seventeen solo exhibitions, has participated in many group shows and is represented in galleries and private collections in South Africa, the United States of America, the United Kingdom and Canada.

She has illustrated eight books, including *The Mantis and the Moon*, by Marguerite Poland, which won the Percy FitzPatrick Prize for Literature and the Sankie Prize, when it was translated into Japanese.

She lives with her artist husband, Harold, on a nature reserve in Mpumalanga, South Africa. They have two sons, Max, an architect, and Walter, an artist and pilot.

THERE ARE TWO *spiritual dangers in not owning a farm. One is the danger of supposing that breakfast comes from the grocery, and the other that heat comes from the furnace. To avoid the first danger, one should plant a garden, preferably where there is no grocer to confuse the issue. To avoid the second, he should lay a split of good oak on the andirons, and preferably where there is no furnace, and let it warm his shins while a February blizzard tosses the trees outside. If one has cut, split, hauled and piled his own good oak, and let his mind work the while, he will remember much about where the heat comes from, and with a wealth of detail denied to those who spend the weekend in town astride a radiator.'*

— ALDO LEOPOLD